# SECURITY CONVERGENCE

# SECURITY CONVERGENCE

## Managing Enterprise Security Risk

**Dave Tyson**

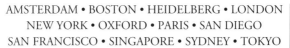

AMSTERDAM • BOSTON • HEIDELBERG • LONDON
NEW YORK • OXFORD • PARIS • SAN DIEGO
SAN FRANCISCO • SINGAPORE • SYDNEY • TOKYO

Butterworth-Heinemann is an imprint of Elsevier

Butterworth-Heinemann is an imprint of Elsevier
30 Corporate Drive, Suite 400, Burlington, MA 01803, USA
Linacre House, Jordan Hill, Oxford OX2 8DP, UK

⊗ Recognizing the importance of preserving what has been written, Elsevier prints its
books on acid-free paper whenever possible.

**Library of Congress Cataloging-in-Publication Data**
Application submitted

**British Library Cataloguing-in-Publication Data**
A catalogue record for this book is available from the British Library.

ISBN 13: 978-0-7506-8425-5

For information on all Butterworth-Heinemann publications
visit our Web site at www.books.elsevier.com

Printed in the United States of America
07  08  09  10  11  12    10  9  8  7  6  5  4  3  2  1

# *Table of Contents*

# *Foreword*

*Security Convergence: Managing Enterprise Security Risk* is about the convergence of security organizations in an institution or commercial enterprise. It provides the first in-depth explanation of the strategy, operations, and tactics for aligning information systems, physical security, corporate security, and related functions in a manner that reduces costs and increases efficiencies for these very important roles, and minimizes the interdependent risks that exist when these functions are not aligned.

The astute reader will recognize that this book is also about organizational change. It emphasizes collaboration and learning to thrive in the corporate security ecosystem of the very near future, which requires security leaders to drive common processes, metrics, and cooperation across otherwise disparate security functions and across all organizations and systems driving the business.

The most successful security leaders today recognize the critical need to integrate security into the business at all levels and through existing processes to be most effective in the long term. Accomplishing those objectives requires the leader to not only be a subject matter expert in all aspects of enterprise security, but also to intuitively and emotionally understand the business, its earnings drivers, and its key success factors.

The first step in true integration is establishing a converged approach to developing an overall security strategy for the organization. Whether all of the security functions report to the same individual or function is irrelevant. This book focuses on the techniques and approaches most successful in meeting the strategic security integration challenge—the convergence of security organizations.

Dave Tyson is eminently qualified to write this book. He has been practicing security convergence for several years. Among other honors, he was dubbed "Mr. Convergence" by *Canadian Security Magazine* and is considered to be one of the thought leaders in the field of security convergence. He is one of the few practitioners to successfully implement convergence in a complex, multistakeholder environment such as the City of Vancouver. He also was recognized by the Alliance for Enterprise Security Risk Management (AESRM) in 2006 as one of the first award winners of the annual Excellence in Security Convergence Award. In 2005, he received the Canadian National Security Pioneer award for his work in the field of convergence.

Our thanks to Dave for undertaking this initial in-depth approach to explaining the process of converging security organizations. It provides insight into what will soon become common practice in corporations and institutions. Dave Tyson will forever be recognized, along with just a handful of other security practitioners, for pioneering the effort.

Timothy L. Williams
Chief Security Officer
Nortel

# *Preface*

The development, introduction, and application of life-changing and disruptive technologies have had a profound effect on society. From the days of the invention of the wheel, to the musket, the automobile, the airplane, the A-bomb, and the Internet—all of these technologies have changed the face of society, impacted people's lives, and altered their environments. The impact of technology on specific industries has varied, with some industries evolving relatively quickly and others lagging behind.

The security profession, in general, has been playing catch-up for 60 years and, although recently some scholars have suggested that the physical security profession's longevity has led to a more refined approach to risk management, this is probably little more than academic speculation. Some have postulated that the field of physical security is better prepared to meet future organizational security challenges because of time-tested strategies and approaches. The reality is more likely that traditional security professionals have seen the gulf between themselves and the evolving security technologies grow over the past 20 years. This divide has driven many physical security practitioners to become specialists in their area of expertise. Although the introduction and adoption of the IT security practitioner by organizations has been glacially slow, it nevertheless has delivered new skill sets to bolster organizations' security postures.

Unfortunately, organizational security was developed in silos and has been implemented in a piecemeal format that led to only one place: gaps of security across the organization. Security professionals know that security is a weakest-link discipline, meaning that wherever a risk goes unmitigated, there exists a weak spot for an incident to occur. As long as there are people factored into the equation, there will be new unidentified and unmitigated risks.

The future for security professionals from all fields of the industry is becoming eminently clearer with every passing month. But as security practitioners perceive this new integrated security continuum, the field of security is becoming more complex with evolving technology, new multifaceted legislation, and a globalizing threat model. The security professional must therefore embrace an enterprise-wide risk management strategy aimed at harnessing organizational resources into a comprehensive approach to risk management and mitigation.

This book is designed to aid all security professionals in more formally exploring the concept of security convergence and providing a platform for discussion about enterprise risk, to begin within departments such as human resources, risk management, internal audit, emergency management, and senior management.

# *Acknowledgments*

To my wife Marilyn for her eternal patience throughout this process, my family for their continued love and support, and my son Logan, who lost out some days when I was writing.

I would also like to thank the following people for their contributions, suggestions, and support during the writing of this book.

Tim williams, Caterpillar

Dave Cullinane, E-Bay

Jeff Spivey, SRG Security Consulting

Ray O'Hara, Vance International

Ed De Lise, the Wackenhut Corporation

Linda Kirksey, Flowserve Corporation

Jim Reavis, ISSA International

Dawson Barber, Drake International

Darryl Braham, St. Paul Traveler's Insurance

Robert Martin, Colgate Palmolive

Dennis Shepp, Shepp Johnman

Mark Zschoch, City of Vancouver

John Gehrlein, Simplex Grinnell

Serge Dupis, Province of Alberta

Pat Hoger, Province of Manitoba

Jim McNeil, Mayo Clinic

Daphne Philos, ASIS International

Thanks also to Roger Fast and Doug Mitchell, my two leaders at the City of Vancouver who have provided significant guidance and support during my time with the City.

Finally, I would like to thank Ian Thompson for his tireless work as a contributing writer and editor.

# *Introduction*

In 1999, I embarked on a new career in the information technology (IT) security field after having spent 16 years in the comfort and safety of the physical security world. I had almost no knowledge about IT, only that of an advanced Microsoft Office user.

My introduction to the field of IT security came while attending an ASIS International luncheon in Vancouver where I met Kirk Baily, a very well-respected IT security professional who led meetings for a group called the Agora in Washington State. The Agora is a group of IT security professionals who meet to discuss and share solutions to the challenges presented by the IT security threats that plague business and government on a daily basis. Kirk encouraged me to attend their next meeting despite my professed lack of IT security knowledge, and thus began my journey into the world of IT security.

At my first Agora meeting, I felt a little out of my league, to say the least, given that I did not know what SPAM or a denial of service (DoS) attack was. But over time, by asking enough questions, I gained a rudimentary knowledge of this other side of security. I realized that I was ready to make the leap into IT because I could clearly see that IT security would not present the frustration that existed in the physical security field, as the physical side only addressed part of the security threats an organization faces. I made contact with a large Canadian IT integrator called the LGS Group, which was looking to hire someone with physical security skills. Specifically, they wanted to be able to offer a fuller service on the physical security side than building data centers for clients. Given my physical security experience, I was a good fit for them, and this was the beginning of my exploration of integrated threat management.

Within a couple of months of my joining LGS, they were acquired by IBM Global Services. Now, my career to this point had consisted of being a bodyguard, a security guard, an investigator, a security consultant, an alarm salesman, and pulling wires through the attic of a house to install an access control system. But this was a completely different world—a world where security jobs are referred to as engagements and everything is process-driven. The company spent thousands of dollars training me in all things IT security, including how security consulting is a process. This was a watershed experience in many ways: The first was when I asked my instructors about the gaps between physical and IT security—the deafening thud of silence that followed that question set my mind in motion regarding the concept of security convergence. I could now clearly see that IT and physical security were different fields with a social, cultural, and physical gulf between them, even though they were dealing with many of the same issues.

Organizational security has generally developed with pockets of risk management responsibilities throughout an organization. Regardless of whether the organization is centralized or decentralized, most organizations have taken a somewhat organic approach to managing the various risks in the organization. Physical security evolved from physical building protections, security guards, personnel protection programs, and special events, to protecting information in filing cabinets, trade secrets, conducting internal investigations, and providing electronic security systems and proprietary surveillance.

IT or information systems security grew from the initial point of wanting to keep important data confidential in stand-alone systems to connecting desktop computers together in the same building. Then businesses began to look toward communicating across local, national, and international geographies. These interconnectivity desires, enabled by the Internet, drove businesses to communicate directly with their customers 24 hours a day, and thus the requisite reliability of computer systems came to be of paramount importance. The evolution of the global village and worldwide corporate mergers and acquisitions created numerous security challenges to interconnect security systems and to provide ubiquitous access to security operational and incident data. The convenience of communicating heterogeneous information nearly instantaneously provided a natural opportunity for the physical security technology manufacturers to leverage their infrastructure and enable global security programs to transform into legitimate enterprise systems.

In this global business world, decentralized security delivery presents an organizational structure ripe for convergence. However, decentralization and a global marketplace are not the only drivers for this change.

The global village, easy 24-hour access to information, increased immigration and societal diversity, and existing worldwide political and cultural conflicts have impacted the threat paradigm for physical security. The security threat paradigm has also been immutably changed by domestic and foreign terrorism. The low-probability, high-impact event is now a reality in our world and must be seriously considered, planned for, and be prepared for through business continuity and emergency management strategies.

Businesses have been affected by more than just the chance of these new threats, so they have to meet head-on these new business realities of this new world. Rising insurance rates have driven organizations to develop more significant risk management strategies. Regulatory compliance requirements have placed more significant, yet nebulous, burdens on those organizations, with a higher level of public trust required. The opportunity for enhanced risk mitigation plays to these business needs.

In a world where the bottom line is often the arbiter of what work gets done, which threats get mitigated, and which controls are put in place, low-cost solutions have a vital role to play. The worldwide nature of business, effective labor mobility, and competition from new markets means that low-cost and effective risk mitigation controls in a competitive business market can be a strategic differentiator for many customer-focused organizations, especially those with a significant stake in maintaining information confidentiality or a high trust relationship with their customer base.

# Security to Date

# 1

# *What is Security Convergence?*

If one accepts the premise that security is a weakest-link discipline, then no organization can truly approach being "secure" unless it considers all of its security risks when crafting overall security strategy and formulating risk mitigation decisions.

For many years, organizations have approached risk mitigation in an essentially siloed format where physical security is managed separately from information technology (IT) security, and separately again from internal audit, privacy, risk and emergency management, and other risk-oriented functions. The gulf between these silos inevitably increases duplication, bureaucracy, and cost.

Over the past few years, business drivers—a global economy and the rate of technical advancement—have compelled these previously independent business functions to become more integrated, to remain cost-competitive, to meet the burdens of new legislation, and to reap operational benefits available from new technologies. This evolution has been termed "security convergence."

A few discrete definitions of security convergence have evolved in recent writings on the topic. A couple examples by writers on the CSO online[1] Web site are:

> [T]he integration of logical, information, physical and personnel security; business continuity; disaster recovery; and safety risk management.

and

> Integrating historically stovepiped functions of operational risk management to achieve better security, oversight of enterprise-wide risk and cost efficiencies.

ASIS International defines convergence as:

> The identification of security risks and interdependencies between business functions and processes within the enterprise and the development of managed business solutions to address those interdependencies.[2]

Although there is probably no one definition suitable for all uses of security convergence, my definition would be:

> Security convergence is the integration, in a formal, collaborative, and strategic manner, of the cumulative security resources of an organization in order to deliver enterprise-wide benefits through enhanced risk mitigation, increased operational effectiveness and efficiency, and cost savings.

Now, with that said, this definition may be a bit overstated only because security convergence can be as much or as little as is useful to an organization.

In practical terms, this activity is about bringing together like-minded people with similar or identical responsibilities for organizational asset protection, and getting them to talk and compare challenges. It has been said that this may initially be best accomplished by informally approaching your colleagues and taking them for a beer or a meal away from the work location. This bottom-up approach will work for many types of organizations whose culture allows for organic growth of ideas. In other organizations, where a top-down style is prevalent, this may be approached through a corporate directive to reduce costs, rationalize resources, or meet legislative responsibilities; either way, convergence can work. To be successful, convergence needs people with the right motivation, the willingness to explore the issues, and then a good plan. All around the world, security professionals have begun to study convergence in more depth and to continue to explore education or training in the sector of security to which they had not previously been exposed. Although still in its infancy, this cross-certification‡ is becoming a reality.

A few writers on convergence have opined that true convergence or integration between security resources in an organization is not advisable or even possible. This seems a safe position to take for consultants or professionals who have not been in the trenches and seen the benefits of true convergence. For those who have converged their business groups and whose organizations are now experiencing the benefits, there is strong evidence that convergence is the future for the security function, whether implemented as a strategic choice by forward-looking security professionals or an action imposed by the organization to meet a business need or changing business environment.

## KEY CONCEPTS OF SECURITY CONVERGENCE

Consider some basic, fundamental key concepts to start the discussion:

1.  Both functions bring strengths to the new relationship.
2.  The groups must learn to speak a common language.
3.  The progress of security convergence needs to be slow and measured.

Both functions (IT security and physical security) bring strengths to the new relationship, and those strengths must be capitalized upon in order to address the inherent challenges in the broader business context. IT security requires technical expertise but not large numbers of staff, whereas physical security generally has the opposite; however, both groups can benefit by uniting their efforts. When these groups work together, the assets of each group can aid in threat mitigation, cost reduction, and improved efficiency throughout the organization.

---

‡Cross-certification: Gaining both physical security and IT security designations.

It is safe to say that, in most organizations, convergence needs to be slow and measured. Introducing any organizational and culture change can be challenging, to say the least; changes with such far-reaching potential impact must be approached methodically. This process must battle historically different hierarchies, dissimilar cultures, and a language gap. Only after the groups begin to speak the common language of risk and begin to work together to improve security can the positive effects can be measured. Once understood and measured, the value of integration must be evangelized throughout the organization to promote continued convergence.

These groups must first learn to communicate in a common language. IT people know very little about patrolling buildings and arresting criminals, whereas physical security people are often equally baffled by firewalls, servers, and viruses. The common language between them is the language of risk. Both groups inform their reporting chain about risk situations that threaten or put at risk the organization's assets, regardless of whether those assets are people, information, or property.

Once this common language has been established, these groups can begin to discuss strategic and tactical issues that plague or threaten the organization, in terms of how they can be mitigated. Only then—once these teams are working together—can convergence begin to occur and its benefits be measured. A good example of this is to consider a proprietary guard force managing the security of a multi-building environment with thousands of employees. The guard force has many small but useful strengths, which can be leveraged to the benefit of the organization. The guards are constantly patrolling the facilities, which gives them an excellent level of knowledge about the normal conditions of the buildings.

Many groups are beginning to engage in security convergence through security industry associations, the vendor community, and formal alliances. Security industry associations have come together to educate members and develop strategic relationships moving forward. Guidelines have been developed for the Chief Security Officer (CSO) position in an attempt to advocate and benchmark the role of the senior security leader in an organization. A separate project exists to define the Chief Information Security Officer (CISO) position. These actions have been taken to educate industry professionals, human resource professionals, and senior management, and to mainstream these relatively new titles and positions.

Industry vendors have developed strategic partnerships similar to the Open Security Exchange Convergence Council, to develop technology to bridge the gap between physical and cyber technology environments. The following quote from the Computer Associates Web site highlights a 2003 study by Pinkerton Consulting and Investigations about collaboration between IT and physical security departments:

> According to a recent research report by Pinkerton Consulting and Investigations, only 36% of all companies surveyed have formal procedures in place for the collaboration between the physical and cyber security departments. The lack of security management results in increased exposure, limited situational awareness, poor accountability and higher operating costs. The Open Security Exchange believes that the interoperability resulting from the use of its specifications will allow organizations to develop formal collaboration between different security functions and will enhance organizational security and operational efficiency.[3]

Convergence engineering, a term recently coined by Shayne Bates of Koffel Associates,[4] refers to the technical issues associated with the integration of logical and physical security. Not so long ago, information security (infosec) vendors protected networks and physical security vendors protected bricks and mortar, and the twain never met. Now that a growing roster of security companies operate in both spaces, as well as in other risk-related areas, we are likely to see an accelerated proliferation of products and security platforms which enable organizations to manage both physical and IT security risks with one product. For example, Brink's Armored Car now offers managed network security services. Unisys, the former mainframe purveyor, has a consulting business in supply chain security. Software giant Computer Associates is collaborating with smart-card vendors such as HID Global Corp. in the Open Security Exchange consortium to develop a network and building access standard called Physbits. Kroll, historically a physical security services provider, now owns Ontrack Data Recovery. Although these are the initial entrants into this new business sector, the market for these products will undoubtedly continue to grow, attracting more and larger manufacturers to the sector.

Probably the most prolific effort to define security convergence mounted to date is the organization created by the International Systems Security Association (ISSA), the Information Systems Audit and Control Association (ISACA), and ASIS International: The Alliance for Enterprise Security Risk Management (AESRM). Created in 2005 to address the management of risks and emerging regulations that require a more thorough, enterprise-wide approach to security, AESRM's purpose going forward is to address issues surrounding the convergence of physical and logical security. AESRM has jointly funded security research on convergence and the effects of convergence on an organization's infrastructure.

## REFERENCES

1.  CSO The resource for security executives Web site. (2005). Available from: http://www.csoonline.com. Accessed October 5, 2005.
2.  ASIS International Web site. (2005). The Alliance for Enterprise Security Risk Management. Convergence of enterprise security organizations. Available from: http://www.asisonline.org/newsroom/alliance.pdf. Accessed October 1, 2006.
3.  Computer Associates Web site. (2005). Press releases. www3.ca.com/Press/PressRelease.aspx?CID=41653. Accessed July 23, 2005.
4.  Koffel Associates, Inc Web site. (2006). Convergence engineering. Available from: www.koffel.com/Convergence%20Engineering.pdf. Accessed October 1, 2006.

# 2

# *Why Should You Care?*

Free trade, the amazingly imprecise mechanism of eliminating or lowering barriers to cross-border trade, has accelerated businesses down the path of expanding the business reach of their organizations. These decisions were often made in a vacuum, with little input from operational departments such as corporate security. Because serious IT security was still a gleam in the eye of a few technology people at that time, global connectivity and supply chain management were developed with functionality, yet limited security, in mind. It was only when the true global businesses started to emerge that security began to be included in discussions such as protecting the supply chain, executive protection while traveling, and intellectual property protection.

The term "global village" was first used by Herbert Marshall McLuhan in the 1960s; in the 1990s this concept evolved to one of worldwide competition, outsourcing of jobs to low-cost countries, and massive mergers. The new business reality of real-time, worldwide connectivity and supply chain management were the orders of the day. Organizations that failed were unable to communicate and operate 24 hours a day, 7 days a week. Many organizations whose core competency did not include global logistics or globally enabled communications were left to scramble to connect and function with disparate technologies and siloed business processes.

The expansion of the Internet and the pandemonium created by the rush to get online and develop e-commerce distribution immutably announced the arrival of the IT security professional, as online businesses failed due to high-profile breaches of customer information. With bandwidth capacity increasingly available, worldwide businesses charged forward, creating larger IT budgets to develop more expansive electronic environments. The electronic data interchange (EDI), which had been the backbone of large organizations' electronic supply chains, was transforming into a customer-centric, end-to-end information system wherein all technology systems ran one centric network. During this time of expansion of the IT security function, the physical security industry had been developing robust, stand-alone access control, closed-circuit television (CCTV), and alarm system technologies that were rapidly transforming their tools to a computer-based workplace.

At the beginning of the twenty-first century, one of the hot topics of discussion was the concept of network convergence. This concept proposed the amalgamation of voice, data, and video over one transmission medium; with it, the idea of leveraging the existing infrastructure for cost savings and enhanced delivery of services was born. Although adoption of this concept has been slow, integrated products have been adopted by many organizations with wide-ranging impacts for their security groups. Voice Over Internet Protocol (VOIP)—the system that replaces your existing telephone system with a system that utilizes a data network to enable an Internet-based telephone system—has received increased adoption worldwide. VOIP is one of the first real, new technologies wherein we see the lines between the security functions being blurred. This new environment created a chasm between how telephone security had been dealt with previously, and how it would have to be dealt with in this new structure.

To further exacerbate the challenges for physical security professionals, global organizations now required a global security solution. The emergence of true enterprise access control, CCTV, and alarm monitoring technology, which run solely on a corporation's data network, created a scenario wherein corporate security professionals were using security technology with no idea of how it really worked or what it was vulnerable to. To compound matters, physical security vendors were selling proprietary, computer-based systems to businesses; those systems were not managed or maintained by corporate IT. This exceptional transformation occurring in the security groups of organizations all across the world inevitably created an environment in which duplicate systems are managed and maintained by siloed security departments.

In a 2005 survey commissioned by the Security Alliance of ASIS International, ISSA, and ISACA, and conducted by the Booze Allen Hamilton research firm, a group of 40 global organizations was surveyed about the business drivers motivating security convergence in their organizations. The top five business drivers were:

- Rapid expansion of enterprise ecosystem
- Value migration from physical to information-based and intangible assets
- New protective technologies blurring functional boundaries
- New compliance and regulatory regimes
- Continuing pressure to reduce cost

## RAPID EXPANSION OF THE ENTERPRISE ECOSYSTEM

Organizations' network environments continue to expand and introduce new and ever-changing risks to the enterprise. Global enterprises connecting disparate systems across countries and continents, connections with third parties, business partners, remote access, wireless, and the connection of back-end legacy systems to the outside world through the Internet are just a few of the examples of processes that seek to extend the perimeter of such organizations.

Mergers, takeovers, and purchases of worldwide companies have created a technical and physical security challenge that has never been faced before. Businesses are conducting commerce worldwide through Web sites and business portals. Often, the customer never actually meets an employee. Instead, a delivery happens via an electronic transaction and an external supply chain partner. From an IT security perspective, this introduces numerous challenges. Electronic transactions enhance the requirement for a robust electronic security system, but increase the opportunity for fraud. It is no longer easy for the corporate security or legal department to do background or credit checks on every customer, as mechanisms to complete this are often unreliable in some countries or are cost-prohibitive. Organizations are continually challenged to provide connectivity to staff who travel. The sales staff wants to access e-mail and sales data from customer locations 24 hours a day, and senior management wants to be able to review strategic information or sensitive documents real-time, in a secure manner, from wherever they are. Operational employees want ubiquitous wireless access to applications for completing their work. All of these business needs drive the perimeter of the business environment farther away from the core assets, and they stress the security mechanisms in place. This push to expand the technology borders of the organization is driving the risk equation to new heights.

In the government sector, the delivery of e-government, 311, and health care integration initiatives are real-world examples of this expansion. E-government is the government equivalent of e-business. Governments are trying to enable taxpayers to engage them in new ways and let taxpayers have more control of how they interact with their government, with greater freedom in acquiring government services. Taxpayers want to buy dog licenses, pay taxes and parking tickets, and vote online without ever having to speak to a civil servant.

The 311 initiative is gaining popularity across North America. This system seeks to connect municipal taxpayers via a single phone call (311) to any nonemergency civic department they need. The implication is a centralized and integrated call center that has access to much of the data held by the local government. This centralization of data creates a new security risk for organizations.

The health care field is another security challenge being driven by a business need to rationalize services and control costs while enabling access to information for a greater number of health care providers and insurance companies. Privacy legislation, such as the Health Insurance Portability and Accountability Act (HIPAA) in the United States and the Freedom of Information and Protection of Privacy Act (FOIPA) in Canada, are examples of this legislation that places a significant burden on organizations to protect patient records and confidentiality. Security providers once only had to worry about patient records stored in filing cabinets, as billing information was mostly all that was kept electronically. Now, most of this information is stored electronically, with some paper backup. The expansion of this enterprise ecosystem has changed much about the way assets have to be protected.

## VALUE MIGRATION FROM PHYSICAL TO INFORMATION-BASED AND INTANGIBLE ASSETS

For many years organizations were primarily concerned with protecting assets in the physical realm. Recently, however, we have seen assets transition from physical records to almost solely electronic form. Records often exist only in electronic format; orthophotos are stored in Geographical Information System (GIS) databases, computer-aided design (CAD) drawings are available online, and critical infrastructure plans and locations can be purchased from Web sites. The assets of organizations that have traditionally been protected in filing cabinets and desks are now found in electronic storage media.

In parallel with the migration of the assets themselves, security professionals have tried to evolve and enhance the skill sets that are required to protect these assets, but technology and vulnerabilities have moved faster than the ability to protect them. With that said, the technology to protect the most common of IT security risks are readily known by IT security professionals, and it is only the resources dedicated to that function that are needed. One of the more common IT security problems is that IT projects are started or systems are purchased without adequate resources being committed to sustaining the project. The world of IT changes rapidly and the risks faced by those systems—whether they are viruses, hackers, or the requirement to integrate into a new business partner— are often left without resources to defend them. It has been said that the IT professional often lacks the communication skills to clearly enunciate the risks, in business terms, to senior management and that this has been the primary cause of business assets not getting the protection they need. This argument has been made by business people about physical security professionals for many years, so it will be crucial for security professionals to become better communicators at the Board room level to ensure that assets are protected throughout the enterprise.

## NEW PROTECTIVE TECHNOLOGIES ARE BLURRING FUNCTIONAL BOUNDARIES

Historically, the tools of the physical security department included the stand-alone access control system, alarm system, and CCTV system. As with all technology, these systems have advanced and become more sophisticated to the point where they now operate solely in the network environment. The interconnectivity that the corporate data network has enabled for IT systems has also facilitated the same integration for the physical security systems.

Security equipment runs on Windows servers, CCTV images are in transit over the data network, and alarm systems report intrusions and fires to the desktop. While this evolution has quietly occurred, physical security professionals have become less knowledgeable about the systems they rely on to conduct their operations. One of the more frightening realities is that physical security equipment is often a proprietary purchase and can be left unsupported over time and actually ends up unpatched, insecure, and open to attack.

Casual surveys of corporate security professionals will often lead to finding they have limited understanding about how to protect their own physical security systems. Given this blurring of the boundaries between the physical and electronic environments, further study will be required to truly understand the implications of these systems interacting in such a codependent manner. One thing is clear: The level of integration is accelerating and being driven by legislative requirements such as Homeland Security Presidential Directive 12 (HSPD-12) in the United States.

The implications of HSPD-12 are a classic example of the functional boundaries of security systems being challenged. The requirement to have all privileges, both physical and technological, managed within one system shows clearly that the previous "demilitarized zone" that existed between the two systems is forever gone. Manufacturers now have a solid government market to justify development of integrated access products. It is likely that this will lead to further advancement in privileges and credential management, and further blur the boundaries between IT and physical security systems.

## NEW COMPLIANCE AND REGULATORY REGIMES

New regulations are enhancing due diligence requirements all over the world. As previously mentioned, the requirements of HSPD-12 are driving convergence in government organizations in the United States. In the private sector, many organizations are required to certify a high level of assurance that their data and financial records are accurate and that personal information is protected. Legislation such as the Personal Information Protection and Electronic Documents Act (PIPEDA) in Canada, and the 2002 Sarbanes-Oxley Act (pertaining to financial and accounting disclosure information), HIPPA, and the 1999 Gramm–Leach–Bliley Financial Services Modernization Act in the United States are all escalating the pressure to efficiently address enterprise security issues.

Given that the requirement is to ensure compliance with legislation and does not deal with the actual form of the data, this drives security professionals to work together to ensure that records are secure and their integrity remains intact.

## CONTINUING PRESSURE TO REDUCE COST

There has been no relief worldwide from the pressure on organizations to do more with less. There are always more projects and initiatives than can be delivered in the public and private sectors. The cost reductions and project cost savings from convergence activities make them attractive to all organizations. Convergence projects offer cost reduction opportunities as well as efficiency bonuses.

## WHY SHOULD YOU REALLY CARE?

If you are a vendor of security products, you should care because convergence offers a new and invigorated market for your products. This new convergence market can bring you new customers or market sectors that you have been previously unable to penetrate. For example, if you were a manufacturer of security alarm reporting consoles that security officers monitor for fire, panic, and physical intrusion alarms, and you expanded that technology to manage alarms from firewall and cyber intrusion detection products, you might be able to open up markets previously unavailable to you. By creating a true network security product that manages all security alarms that travel across the network, customer organizations could cut major operating, employee, and maintenance duplication costs. Although this is only an example, manufacturers should see this as a starting point for discussions of new product opportunities in this converged market.

- According to Forrester Research, in 2006 North American companies will spend $1.7 billion on projects that combine traditional physical security and IT security—more than five times as much as they spent in 2004.[1]
- According to the Stanford Washington Equity Research Group, the forecasted market size for convergence ID card solutions will be more than $12 billion dollars in 2007.[2]

If you are a security services provider or consultant, you should care because convergence provides you with an opportunity to strategically differentiate yourself. The security services market is, in many jurisdictions, swamped with a plethora of undistinguishable providers who offer very little difference from the hundreds of similar vendors. Although guard and alarm companies say they are *different* from their competition, much of this is little more than hyperbole and a fascination with their own marketing material. The fact is that these suppliers all choose from the same gene pool and face the same financial constraints; the only true constant in much of the industry is mediocrity. Now, with this said, there are some superior services out there, but it is difficult to find opportunities for these firms to set themselves apart from the masses. Convergence offers many such opportunities.

Imagine training your contract guard force to locate and report IT security vulnerabilities while they are patrolling the interiors of your buildings. Or imagine physical security consultants who, when conducting risk assessments of building spaces, address *all* of the risks in the physical space, such as rogue wireless access points, live computer jacks in public spaces, or insecure computer rooms. Such services would be significantly value-added and would allow the provider to show true enterprise expertise regarding the risks their clients are facing. Again, although these are just examples, they should start the conversation going. The only cost of implementing these services is some education; the marginal cost of deploying the service is virtually zero.

If you are a leader for security in an organization, you should care because convergence means cost savings, efficiency in mitigating risk, and enhanced organizational effectiveness. Although security convergence means different things to different people, the one thing that remains constant is the opportunity to rationalize security activities and save costs. Convergence is one of those activities that needs to be nurtured and allowed to happen organically, if possible. If convergence is given the opportunity to grow and address organizational challenges, the cost savings will be realized. For example, in one organization there was to be a large expenditure on a dedicated fiber network to run a secure tunnel for CCTV imagery to travel from camera positions to a regional control center; the cost of this dedicated network was estimated at $2 million in fiber alone. Given that this network was to be a duplicate of the existing data network, this was a prime opportunity for convergence to work. The challenge was in securing the CCTV images while they were in transit but to not significantly impact network bandwidth. The physical security staff were completely unaware that alternate solutions were available and were working hard to justify this expense. But as the team worked together, they discovered that a virtual local area network (VLAN)‡ could allow the images to travel securely across the data network without the $2 million capital outlay. Many other cost saving opportunities are available in convergence, including some possible staff rationalization, server consolidation, and so forth. It requires only the willingness to look for these types of savings.

Efficiency in mitigating risk offers a great value to organizations. Management must contend with many activities in reviewing risk information and making risk decisions, including reviewing risk-related metrics, getting updates from security personnel on security issues, and allocating time for security awareness presentations across the organization. In a converged world, these functions can be done once and only once. Instead of reviewing two security

---

‡Virtual local area network (VLAN): A method of securely segmenting traffic flowing across a network.

metrics reports or having presentations by two security departments and then having to integrate the risks of both presentations, leaders can now get one report document or presentation that provides a snapshot of all security risks across the organization. I am sure that leaders of an organization would see a definite benefit in having significant time freed up to deal with other matters. Further, those same leaders can make better decisions when they understand the entire security picture and do not have to prioritize the risk information themselves.

One of the best risk mitigation activities an organization can engage in is conducting security awareness sessions with management and staff. Both physical security and IT security need to get awareness information to staff on an ongoing basis. So if your organization has two awareness or education programs, the ability to combine them into one saves the organization time and money. If an organization has a defined physical security orientation and/or awareness training session, but does not have IT security awareness, an opportunity is created to retrain presenter staff to deliver the IT security message at no additional (or marginal) cost. Although these are all just examples, they are real-world and have been employed at organizations that are receiving these benefits. Leaders need to see these benefits and encourage their security staff to educate themselves and drive the resulting benefits through the organization.

## REFERENCES

1.   Scalet, S.D. (2005). Convergence: Case study. Security 2.0. Available from: www.csoonline.com/read/041505/constellation.html. Accessed October 5, 2005.
2.   Grant, J. Identity solutions industry report. (2006). Washington, DC: Stanford Washington Equity Research Group.

# 3

# *Cultural Differences*

Ask any informed security professional (either physical security or IT security) about the debate over security convergence and reporting structure, and he or she will likely tell you that the *other* side should report to them when discussion about converging the two groups begins. The problem is, frankly, that both types see themselves as professionals in what they do, and do not understand the other side's culture well enough to feel comfortable about reporting to them in a chain of command.

In my interviews for this book, I asked many security professionals from both sides of the aisle how important it was for them to get a better understanding of the other group's culture. The answer that rang through almost universally is that this is critical if this convergence idea is going to work and deliver long-term value to the organization. So, to best approach explaining the differences, let us start by first breaking down the cultures.

## SOCIAL DIFFERENCES

To be frank again, these two groups grew up differently. Where they come from on a career path, the type of professional development they engage in, and even some of their hobbies are significantly different. The physical security professional typically developed because there was a need to physically protect society from the dangers of an expanding and exceedingly complex world. Although private security can trace its roots to the days of the "watch and ward" system in England, I would say that the impetus for the growth of the modern private security industry has been only over the past 60 years or so.

The tenets of the physical security world are about the protection of people, information, and property. Physical security people often come from law enforcement or were private investigators, executive protection specialists, alarm salesmen, camera installers, or even security guards. Some of these jobs are more glamorous than others; the physical security person who did not come from law enforcement probably wore a uniform at one point and had some pretty nasty jobs. Try to imagine standing beside a large pile of sand for 12 hours a day for a week, ensuring that nobody makes off with it. Or, worse, guard a large hole in the ground to ensure that nobody comes along and falls into it. Wow, this is exciting stuff! My first guard job in the security business was guarding a marina; this was relatively okay, except that a winter's day on the water is cold and pretty unpleasant. I remember one job where I was part of a team guarding the outside of an art gallery. We just walked around it for eight hours a day, engaging the local street youth. Every time we walked away they would start dealing drugs and skateboarding until the instant we came back and asked them to stop. This cycle of frustration is less prominent in jurisdictions with property trespass legislation, which enables people to be arrested for habitual trespass acts; however, this was not the case in my jurisdiction. As a security guard, bodyguard, or anyone else protecting something or someone, you encounter some people who will try to impose their importance as a way to gain privilege. Most physical security people will tell you of their joy at hearing someone say, "Do you know who I *am*?" To understand the culture, try to imagine having no viable employment opportunities except for wearing a polyester outfit, having people spit at you and call you names, and then—when you do your job—watch them walk away laughing because they know someone who will let them go. This is what I call working your way up through the physical security industry.

The law enforcement officer who makes the successful change into corporate security has a similar but different history. It certainly does not improve your outlook when you find yourself dealing with a domestic disturbance for the tenth time, arresting the same shoplifter again and again, or chasing down the never-ending parade of drug dealers, only to have a judge let them out before the paperwork is done. These security folks have been lied to by just about everyone they have ever come across in their professional careers, and often this has a lasting effect on them. I have hired many former police officers in my career, and the ones who are successful in the corporate security world are the people who are still passionate about the job.

I guess that it is really the physical security professionals who are passionate about protection. In my experience, they tend to be more conservative than most, which probably comes from a clear understanding of managing risk. These people tend have a "Not on my watch" belief system. In my experience, this is the most powerful attribute a security professional can have—the personal credibility and responsibility to take ownership of a situation and see that it is resolved correctly, and to make sure that people's lives, information, and property are protected. This is what defines a dedicated security professional. I have been witness to countless security guards working extra hours, aiding someone in need on the street—giving money from their own pocket—just because they were there and it was "their watch."

Physical security tenets are old and established; they are relatively well-known in society, and most people understand that locking doors and windows is a must-do thing in most cities around the world. Generations of physical security veterans have retired and, until recently, this industry was thought to be a mature industry by many people's standards.

Conversely, IT or information systems (IS) security is a relatively new field in the scope of the past 100 years or so. The modern desktop computer has been around for only a generation or so, and the development of the dedicated IT security professional community has followed suit with this expansion. IT security grew up as a needs-driven specialty within the IT environment. The centralization of data and computing power combined with the newfound reliance of business on the automation of the business process, forcing most organizations to acknowledge the inherent risk. Specialization in security created an entire new industry, a lot of which was based on protecting the data and technical systems from outside intrusion.

IT security professionals are new and highly technical. They understand systems well and see the problem of security as a matter of hardware and software, with the problem of people interacting with the technology. As I mentioned in the Introduction, my first job in IT security was as a physical security professional with the LGS Group, a mid-market IT integrator. The view of a person I now consider to be the visionary leader of the time, Steve Schnider, was that you cannot secure a data center or computer server room without involving the physical security function. He was so right!

I asked a lot of questions then, and began to evolve into the culture of an IT security person. Over the next five years, I began to think more like an IT person, pondering interfaces between technology, and transactions where there are no human interactions. You know that you are talking to a true techie when they personalize the equipment and refer to the technology as he or she. I was highly confused when talking to network engineers and they were talking about "he" is not doing this or that. When I sheepishly asked whom they were referring to, I discovered they were referring to this 20-pound chunk of metal and printed circuit boards as "he."

I have found that the true IT security professional sees security as a process—the way it should be seen. I had been in the security industry for nearly two decades, but it was not until I entered the IT security industry that I saw what a standards-based approach and formal security methodology could do for an organization.

My introduction to this was the now somewhat famous IT security wheel, shown in Figure 3-1. This wheel crystallized in one image for me that security is a process and I, in an instant, knew what could be improved upon in the physical security world to increase mitigation for building security, risk assessments, security reviews, etc.

The tenets of the IT security world are about ensuring the confidentiality, availability and integrity of data.

- *Confidentiality:* Seeks to ensure that only authorized parties get access to data.
- *Availability:* Seeks to ensure that computer systems and data are available and their function is uninterrupted.

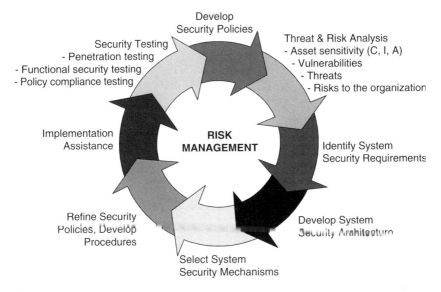

**Figure 3-1**   Security wheel.

- *Integrity:* Seeks to provide quantitative proof that a message or data has not been modified in an improper way, either intentionally or accidentally.

IT security professionals work to create an environment that can be counted on to provide technology and data with 99.999% availability. Everyone knows how frustrating it is to not be able to access your e-mail or the Internet. If your organization relies on its data systems to earn revenue or save lives, the cost of downtime, incorrect information, or exposure of sensitive data can have grave consequences. This creates a situation where these security professionals need repeatable, reliable, and verifiable results. Therefore, processes such as security methodologies and standards-based approaches have gained huge success in this environment. Essentially, you can probably check this off as a quality control approach to delivering a high level of assurance that systems are secure and available.

My next IT security epiphany came when I was introduced to the BS 7799 IT security standard, shown in Figure 3-2. This model enabled me to start thinking about security as a weakest-link discipline, which I now believe wholeheartedly. Many in the industry decried the reliance on such a generic, high-level benchmark. But, once again, I had never before seen such an approach and such a useful tool. I immediately translated this model into the physical security world, and thanked my IT security counterparts for being so smart and process-oriented about security. Now, I am not saying that physical security does not have elements of these ideas embodied in the field, but I think the examples are confined to more high-security environments. These are more process-based environments because physical security is operationally based, and can be about saving lives and protecting national assets at this level. I personally have just not seen as much of this in the commercial market as I have in IT security.

IT has had a more robust approach to the process of security, and has marketed itself well as the enabler of business. Figure 3-3, from the days of the dot com, depicts how IT security sold itself to organizations—as the business enabler.

Many IT security professionals have come from more general IT backgrounds. They were programmers, software specialists, or computer hardware builders. Probably the most common background is that of the network administrator. This is the person who

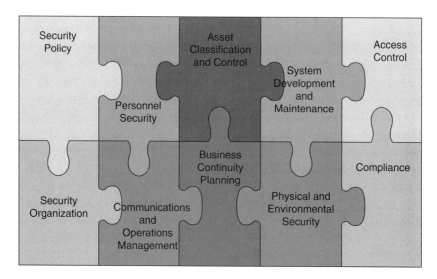

**Figure 3-2**  Security management model.

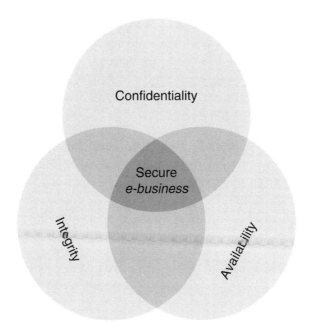

**Figure 3-3**  IT security marketing approach.

(in most organizations) is tasked with issuing rights to the users on the network. This is an access control function, which is at the core of any security system. There is nothing like poring over 20,000 electronic records or lines of data to motivate you to come up with a more automated way of doing things, or doing password policy compliance reviews to make you a little frustrated. Sitting down with a list of cracked passwords and determining who each person is, so that you can go explain to them why choosing a more complicated password is a good idea, gets old in a hurry. It is actually very similar to how I felt after 10 years of telling people to lock up their valuables—tired!

Now I will not say that IT security people are not passionate about what they do, because I have met many who are. But let us just say that there are situations where the technology does not evoke the same level of unbridled passion as chasing down a wifebeater and slapping the cuffs on. The first generation of IT security veterans are probably considered baby boomers and are now ready to retire. They are the people of the 1960s, 1970s, and 1980s who embraced technology. They are also likely to have some pretty cool technology in their homes.

- There are many similarities between physical security and IT security groups.

Security professionals from both fields will be happy, or dismayed, to know that many of their challenges, frustrations, and inspirations are similar in both groups. My experience has been that both fields are faced with the following challenges.

## Reactive Business Leadership

Business leaders are often very reactive in their approach to security measures meant to mitigate threats. After the Oklahoma City bombing, a link was made to a previous visit of one of the suspects to the city of Vancouver, Canada. It was the lead story on the news that day, and I would estimate that static guard coverage increased 10% across the city for the next few days. I heard from seven guard firms that were desperate to find extra staff to service their short-term needs. Now remember, this was a link from months before the bombing occurred, yet businesses were reacting to the possibility that this news story could deliver a higher level of risk. While I was with IBM's Canadian Security and Privacy practice, a software vulnerability was announced in the news and the story emerged about the loss of customer data from one large organization in the United States. We were bombarded with requests for quotations for risk assessments and security reviews to determine the security posture of these requesting companies. Less than 10% of those engagements were ever actually completed by us. After a few days, the customers seemed to lose interest in the risk. The interesting part is that the vulnerability being discussed had been publicly known for more than two years and the fix (patch) had been available by free download for more than 18 months.

As I mentioned in Chapter 2, the ability to effectively communicate security risk to senior management, in business terms, is crucial for success. It would seem easy to say to management that there are insufficient resources available to complete the patching of critical servers and that because of this, customer or crucial company information is at risk, which could lead to a massive embarrassment to the organization or a loss of business. Frequently, the problem is that security practitioners on both sides of the fence practice a communication technique called fear, uncertainty, and doubt (FUD).

## The Sky Is Falling

FUD has been the main tool employed by security professionals for many years. Often, our business leaders will only be scared into action by "The sky is falling" statements; even then, this is often all the security professionals can do to mitigate the risk. Most security professionals I know will tell you the aspect they most hate is selling security on the premise that "If you do not do this, the world is over tomorrow." We would all like to make a strong business case for security and have it taken seriously on its own merits. I personally made the effort to come up with a model called the Security Value Chain,[1] an entirely new way to communicate the value that security creates in an organization and its impact to the profitability of the organization. It has been since revised and is discussed in Chapter 24. Another security management magazine would not publish it as it was too theoretical for them. I guess it did not have the imperative of "The sky is falling."

## Being the Last to Know

Security people are often some of the last to know about security requirements. In many situations they are asked to create a "bolt-on" solution at the last minute. Security practitioners will mostly agree that security needs to be designed into most situations on Day One, not added on later. The anecdotal number I hear quoted is that the cost to design IT security during the architecture stage of a project is only 10% of what it would be to retrofit security after the system is built. For example, while I was at the LGS Group we were asked to design the security for an e-marketplace. This is a dot-com concept for centralized shopping, like an online shopping mall. This was going to accept credit card transactions online in real time. The application was essentially built and, when the designers came to the security group, I told them the bolt-on solution was likely going to be a public key encryption (PKE) solution and it would cost somewhere between $500,000 and $2 million to build, given that there was very little inherent security built in and it was built on an older Microsoft platform. Given that the entire project had cost $3 million, *they were not impressed!*

In 1992, I was in charge of security for a conference center and the entire venue had been booked for three large functions. The three different event coordinators had dutifully booked the events, and at our monthly security meeting never mentioned a word about the nature of the groups. When my security staff and I arrived, three of us were booked to provide coverage for the special event, one for each group; we were a little surprised (to say the least) to learn the groups' identities. You see, there was a little conflict growing in Eastern Europe at the time and some pretty hard feelings existed between the groups, but they were going to share a social celebration period. The three groups—Bosnians, Croats, and Serbs—were filing into their respective rooms and the conference center then proceeded to sell them lots of alcohol and asked them to use the same restroom facilities. Does anyone see the problem here—three security guards and 4500 emotionally charged and inebriated guests? We got out of this without a scratch, or a punch being thrown, but it was immediate and drastic action that got it done. Why was security last to know?

Both IT and physical security groups work hard every day to mitigate risk, identify threats, and build countermeasures to protect people, information, and property. They both face the task of convincing management, business units, stakeholders, and the public that it is better to advise security up-front, and more cost effective when it comes time to deliver the security solution.

## Much of What Is Done Today in Security Came from the Military

Many of the physical and IT security tools and technologies that are the mainstay of a professional security operation today came from military applications in years gone by. Modern encryption systems were developed during war time to protect messages in transit between the battleground and command locations. Today, encryption is used in many business environments to protect sensitive company data and electronic transactions. Electronic commerce is built on the premise that the transaction can be authenticated to one particular person and the integrity of the content is valid.

CCTV technology has been developed over the years by governments to conduct reconnaissance on other countries from space and mobile platforms such as planes and airborne drones. Many of these technologies have found their way into physical security equipment in the form of infrared and low-light-visibility camera lenses.

## They Like to Tell War Stories

Physical security people and IT security people, although significantly different, are amazingly similar. On a recent business trip to an IT security conference, I spent an evening with IT security professionals from around the United States, having dinner and talking shop. Inevitably, it came around to the time of the evening where the "war stories" come out. I was regaled with stories from some large organizations about the ridiculous situations we see in the security business—wireless devices being plugged into networks and used with no regard for the risk; entire networks compromised when another organization plugged their network into an insecure router; and many more. It reminded me of my physical security days when the daily routine included telling the stories of the foolishness we saw that day—the crazy, naked woman walking through the shopping mall; the guy driving the stolen car and leaving his wallet inside; and all the other Darwin Award winners the security staff are forced to deal with. I guess this is true enough of many industries, but it made me feel reassured to see the similarities and shared experiences we have.

## PHYSICAL SECURITY DEPARTMENTS

In general, physical security groups are often not well trained. Organizations far too often put security personnel on the front lines of the organization with minimal training, often leaving it to the government jurisdiction to set minimum standards that must be followed. It has often astounded me how easily organizations hand over responsibility of their assets after hours to some of the least-understood and -supported folks in the business. Security groups are plagued with limited budgets when it comes to security personnel and often need to outsource this service to contract security firms.

Physical security staff generally work well with rules, but those firms often do not create many of them unless absolutely necessary. Post orders or standing operating procedures are generally what you will find. They are not as likely to create and document standards and processes, do benchmarking, or create business cases, but they do bring a risk management culture to the table that IT does not generally have; they are natural risk assessors and managers.

I recently purchased a software package targeted at the physical security industry. It took me a year to build the business case for this technology because none of the sales people at this international organization could translate the features of their product into business value. They could tell me what it did but not what the business benefits and return on investment quotients were. The culture and commoditization of the industry has created a marketplace driven by relationship-based sales. This is different from the IT security world (which is discussed later) in that, in most cases, customers are buying these services on a regular basis and the products and services differ little in approach. This is not to deny that some products are more technically sophisticated than others, but in general terms they are commoditized and well understood by the customer base. This may be because of the fact that they are often less specialized and therefore purchased by more of the market. Although intrusion alarms have been an essential tool of big business for years, the home alarm market has exploded over the past 20 years, introducing more and more people to the technology and to the comfort level that comes with it.

The evolution that physical security professionals must complete will be challenging because, although they are hard-working and dedicated, the external technology risk factors facing them today are just beginning. Their culture will need to progress to one that embraces change and technology and can begin to acquire a modicum understanding of technology and how it affects and exposes the organization to risk.

## INFORMATION TECHNOLOGY SECURITY DEPARTMENTS

My first thought when becoming truly aware of the IT world was that it is an environment that succeeded because of "smoke and mirrors." So much of what I found and learned had been shrouded in a veil of secrecy made up of buzzwords and technobabble. Although the security function is very similar in nature to IT, it has been segmented from other security functions by the terminology and technology complexity. In truth, the activities of access control, authentication, risk assessment, and investigations are as common in IT security as they are in physical security.

IT security people, in general, have a much greater understanding of process and standards in security because that is the fundamental basis of the technology environment. Application development is cyclical; each time something is created, servers and computers are, at least theoretically, built and deployed the same way each time. IT has embraced the value of being able to repeat results as a measure of creating efficient value within the organization. One could easily argue, though, that security convergence has caught many IT security professionals a little off guard; over the past 20 years, physical security systems have steadily become more automated and reliant upon computers. On the other hand, the typical IT security person cared very little about physical security until recently, when faced with CCTV systems intruding on their network and consuming large volumes of bandwidth.

But it is interesting to note the difference between the approaches to selling IT security, as it is quite different from the relationship-driven physical security industry. The sales process in the IT security market is much more project- and product-centric. This technology-centric approach is about access to the expertise and technology that will better enable your business and protect many of your intangible assets. This creates an environment where many buyers have limited expertise in purchasing these services and often have limited technical understanding of the details of what will occur. A vulnerability assessment of a network, performed by an ethical hacker, involves the attempted penetration of the businesses IT systems by a skilled specialist. These skills are neither common nor easily understood. Few people purchase these services and, for those who do, these are generally not regular purchases (often only annually or less frequently).

The classic IT security sales process usually involves a sales person contacting a potential customer in a position such as mine, to explain how their product or service can solve my problem. This is an epidemic in the IT world—the vendor does not really want to know me or my business problems; they simply want to push their technology. I often have three or four different representatives calling me every year from each company, whereas my representative from the physical security vendors has not changed in years. Now I am not sure if this is a good or bad thing, but if these cultures are going to learn to work together, they will need to overcome this difference.

Although most security professionals reside in one of these two silos, a small proportion grew up in both worlds or made the switch, and these professionals are today's security convergence thought leaders. They understand that the security professional who can speak both IT and physical security parlance, can understand the value of processes, standards, and business cases, and can culturally lead both groups will succeed with the challenges to be faced by organizations in the future. These people are most likely to become the first generation of security convergence veterans in the years to come.

Right now every business group, especially risk groups, seems to think it should report to the CEO. Although I do not disagree that security needs to report higher up in the organization, it would be easier to make the case if the two groups could report through one process, if not one voice.

## REFERENCE

1.  Tyson, D. (2004), The security value chain. *Canadian Security Magazine*, March 2003, 25(2):32–33; April 2003, 25(3):24.

# *The Changing of the Guard*

# Changing the Threat Paradigm

**4**

Implicit in all discussions about the security risks organizations face today is the changing threat paradigm that now confronts the world. For many years, the physical security department had been chiefly responsible for dealing with organizational responses to acts such as fraud, theft, and harassment in the workplace. However, the advancing importance of technology in business has necessitated new people in the organization being given the responsibilities for security activities. In the past, these IT security practitioners usually worked in isolation and had very little involvement with the traditional security practitioner. Combine this with the lack of an organizational imperative to work together, and you create a gulf between groups responsible for both risk assessment and mitigation in the organization. Then add poor intergroup communications, varied backgrounds, and unconnected vertical reporting structures, and you get a siloed approach to security and create holes in the enterprise security posture.

The complexity of the technical environment creates a different kind of ecosystem within which security professionals function. In the physical world, we see mostly discrete acts that are either discovered or not discovered, with an eventual understanding of the cause and effect. Conversely, in the computer world there can be many combining factors involved in understanding the loss event. In fact, it may be many system or component breakdowns that lead to an eventual security compromise. This kind of creeping incrementalism combines one weakness with another until the vulnerability is exposed and exploited. For example, it can be difficult to determine how someone's password was compromised:

- Was it a piece of spyware downloaded to the computer that collected the password?
- Was a virus introduced to the system because a patch was not applied or an antivirus software update was not completed?
- Or did a coworker get unrestricted access to the computer and acquire the password locally?

It is difficult to identify the exact cause. There are parallel scenarios in the physical world, because not all losses are discrete events. For example, we can examine a retail or office environment that has had a plummeting level of morale or workplace loyalty; this often results from a change in management style, labor unrest, or lack of relative wage parity with other organizations. Now add limited internal controls on assets, lack of surveillance systems, or lack of formal access controls so employees can move about undetected at any hour. Top this off with infrequent inventory reconciliations and you have a perfect environment for internal theft. Although you may have difficulty identifying what the cause for the loss would be, the creeping incrementalism of neglecting the management of security controls leads to a loss event with no audit trail.

The grey areas between the physical security and the IT security departments are where the organization is often most vulnerable! In many organizations, the convergence points[‡] are often left

---

[‡]Convergence point: The point where physical and IT security risks connect or cross over in the organization.

unguarded or left to the protections afforded by non-security professionals. Often, telecommunication systems are managed by IT people or administrators, wiring closets are managed by facilities personnel, and social engineering threats are managed by no one. The new technology and new electronic transportation mechanisms enabled by interconnectivity create a foreign world for traditional security professionals.

The threat paradigm facing business has changed over the past few years. Arguably, external business security threats have had three paradigm shifts around the world in the twenty-first century. The first happened on September 11, 2001 when the low-probability, high-impact event became a very clear reality. Business contingency plans and risk management strategies rarely entered the upper right-hand quadrant of the risk matrix shown in Figure 4-1.

This was a call to arms for senior management to review and understand their aggregate organizational risk. Low-probability, high-impact events are a reality, and cracks in the security program enable them.

The second paradigm shift occurred with the introduction of robust legislation designed to place significant accountability on senior management for the protection of financial and personal information held by an organization. This new legislation, such as

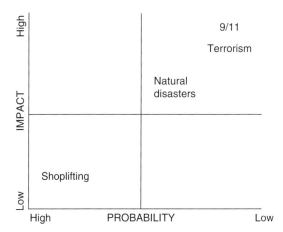

**Figure 4-1**   Security risk matrix.

the Sarbanes-Oxley Act in the United States or country-specific privacy acts, has prescribed penalties (including substantial fines or even jail sentences) for data loss or integrity violations. This is a salient departure from traditional accountability, because now the persons arguably farthest from the controls and often with the least technical knowledge of the asset's protection are at most risk of personal loss if the controls are insufficient.

The third shift occurred in a much less dramatic, albeit more significant, manner. The velocity of crimes and business risk was changing at an unprecedented rate (in a gradual manner over the past two or three years), and conventional security practitioners were faced with a new foe that left a new type of evidence trail. Historically, practitioners had used traditional investigative and security process tactics to hunt down the culprit and initiate further punitive action. In the virtual business world, these crimes can occur with stealth, anonymity, and blinding speed, and can eviscerate any protections the physical security department can employ. The traditional security professional is often left unprepared to deal with cyber stalking, viruses that introduce spyware and keystroke loggers to an employee's computer, or the theft of an employee's identity through electronic means. These profitable and destructive behaviors can add significant stress to a workplace environment and place new burdens on IT security personnel who have traditionally had their responsibility limited to technology and data protection.

Given these new tools, organized crime has expanded its reach to cyber crime. The Internet was not designed with security in mind, and many organizations' IT security maturity is still low. This facilitates a robust opportunity for criminals to engage technology and tactics to profit from and use for mass information gathering for people-oriented crimes. IT security people have for years asserted to senior management that major security changes need to be implemented, often at the cost of convenience or competing projects. In many organizations, this sage and forward-looking advice was treated as either fear-mongering or prescriptive twaddle. Through security convergence, security groups can unify their security messages and deliver more cost-effective security controls to meet this new security threat paradigm.

# 5

# *Changing the Security Environment*

One of the key challenges to security as a discipline is that security is an imprecise solution to an ill-defined problem. There are virtually no absolutes in security, and it is almost always a case of a best effort to reduce, but not eliminate, risk. Further, security practitioners are often subject to new governance structures and changing priorities for security in the organization's makeup.

Let us start by examining the continuum of effectiveness that different security mechanisms have for securing assets. Adding up the receipts in a cash register and comparing that to the day's inventory will give you a reasonably reliable picture of how that function performed during that period of time. The problem is that this assumes that all the products were actually rung into the register originally, so identification of this weakness is where we must begin to build an array of security processes to protect the assets—the cash and the products. So we add CCTV to watch the staff and customers; inventory control to reduce shrinkage of inventory; access control and audit logs to track the transactions on the point of sale (POS) or electronic cash register device; and other mechanisms to reduce the risk of losses. Nevertheless, losses somehow continue to occur because threats to the assets are constantly changing and, as mentioned in Chapter 3, security staff are often last to know about changing business conditions. Consider whether the inventory control system that was installed utilizes radio frequency identification (RFID) technology with no security controls engaged, as this could create a way for hackers to access the computer POS device and possibly attack the integrity of the inventory data. If the attacker can change the inventory numbers in the database, he or she is free to remove the product from the warehouse without fear of deficits in the inventory reconciliation.

Another common security practice is reconciling the people who enter and exit a building with the security events in the building, and the external factors present at that time; this tells you very little (with absolute certainty) about what this process is trying to protect. The challenge here is that most people design security systems from the outside in (assuming, of course, that threats from the outside represent the largest risk to the organization's assets, which we know is patently untrue—the majority of losses have at least an insider element to them, if they are not outright committed by an insider). This trend is only increasing and will continue to become more acute as computer systems become more interconnected across the organization.

The advent of converged identity management products and Internet protocol (IP) addressable door hardware are two examples of the changing security environment that security practitioners from both sides of the aisle have to face when looking at how their environment is changing. Questions will arise in this new environment, such as who will administer the new converged identity management system. If you are in a jurisdiction where standards exist surrounding the background and reliability of the individuals who are tasked with this role, this may not be such a problem for you. But for others who have bargaining unit members whose collective agreements do not currently allow for stringent personal integrity checks, this may raise some system integrity issues. I am not saying that union members are a problem; what I am saying is that when you begin to converge identity information from your physical and IT environments, you are aggregating all privileged information in one location. Therefore, the value of the asset has increased and the risk of exposure may also have similarly incrementally increased. Likewise, when you begin to deploy IP addressable door hardware and system access, you can now allow an attacker to release security locking mechanisms or reprogram the unlock schedules. The security environment has changed drastically.

This imprecise set of controls is deployed because many security professionals are working under the assumption that we cannot mitigate the unknown. Hence, we put general security protection systems (access control, cameras, alarms, and security guards) in place and hope they can protect us from the risks. We are therefore working with an ill-defined potential problem and a general or imprecise solution. The convergence or the aggregation of all of the organization's security requirements "earns its pay" when you look at this security challenge and accept that you cannot remove all risk from the equation, but you can optimize the risk. By including the security controls, you as a practitioner understand that you can mitigate many of the risks, but what about the risks from the threats you do not fully understand? My experience has been that many practitioners are not aware of some of the threats that exist in their own security systems. So the primary idea to take away from this discussion is that *convergence is about optimizing the risk profile* so that all risks are identified, considered, and either mitigated or accepted—ideally with some form of compensating control. I urge you to truly ponder this thought in detail: *identify and mitigate ALL the risks in the environment.* This is what the convergence security practitioner, or group of practitioners, must do. Senior management should not be accepting any more risk than they are aware of, and if all the risks are well understood in this new and increasingly complex environment, then the first part of the job is done.

Now, add to this equation the possibility of the low-probability, high-impact event, and that each organization is in the predicament of trying to determine whether their establishment could be impacted by such an event. The difficulty is that even though catastrophic events seem to occur with increasing frequency around the world, the security function can have only limited effect in addressing the risks. Security can generally only respond to the events and mitigate or reduce the impact the event has on the organization. Given that this is a best-effort process, security groups need to maximize any advantages or tools they have available to them. There is a definite need to share intelligence and threat data across the organization as well as external to the organization. An increase in the theft of laptops, for example, can have significant implications for the IT infrastructure and the security of the network, and increased suspicious calls to the help desk may indicate potential social engineering activity that the firm may be subjected to.

The velocity of data movement in organizations seems to be escalating and businesses have begun to track every aspect of their relationship with their customers. They aggregate, sell, share, and analyze customer data with increased fervor. Customer data is the life blood of many organizations, and failure to protect it can bring down the business. Legislation in many jurisdictions requires businesses to inform customers of personal data losses. In many cases, these data losses lead to customer losses for those companies.

It is not always as simple as customer data being obtained through a Web server or a database being hacked; there have been numerous occurrences of laptops being stolen from employees' cars and homes, as well as hard drives or backup tapes being stolen while in normal transit. The risks to customer data are no longer a simple matter of IT security protections; there is also a physical component to its protection. When servers are preloaded with a company's image and shipped via courier across the country, or a hard drive backup tape is taken off-site for storage, a very real physical risk is created. This new security environment is one where IT and traditional security professionals need to cooperate and pool their expertise to protect the organization's assets.

## THE THREATS HAVE CONVERGED

Beside the fact that businesses are changing their systems and exposing their assets to increasingly more complex security risks, the external environment is changing at an accelerated pace. Internet technologies and free, open-source, software programs make it relatively easy for people to acquire or build malicious electronic tools. These tools are important to security practitioners because they can be used to commit crimes or annoying and expensive acts against your business, customers, or personnel. It is important for practitioners to understand how these tools are used and how they can affect an organization's environment. Although much of this could be discussed between your IT and physical security staff members over a beer after work, I will give a brief review of some of the more common tools of the malicious trade.

Although I do not have the statistics handy, it is not far off to say that identity theft is probably the number one target for criminals on the Internet. The electronic collection of personally identifiable data has been a booming industry in recent years and makes the process of identity theft much easier to commit. Many years ago, when identity theft was confined to the physical world, all criminals had to do was steal mail from your mailbox or sort through your garbage to get access to the information they needed. Now they can capture many of the pieces of information they need right off your computer. People often store important details about themselves, such as their Social Security or Social Insurance numbers, driver's license, scanned copies of birth certificates, and other information, right on their computers; often it is in the form of electronic tax returns that contain much of the information thieves need to steal your identity. Add to that the businesses that maintain credit card numbers in POS systems or in databases with limited controls on the access, or limited background screening on the employees who have access to the information—I have even heard stories of businesses using prison labor to process the personal information of customers.

Another all-too-common use of technology is employees or domestic acquaintances who use new technology for harassment or stalking purposes. If someone can get access to a workstation or laptop, and adequate security controls are not in place, then it is quite easy to install a keystroke logger on the target computer. This logger will log every keystroke made by users and then surreptitiously transfer this file off the computer to the person who installed it. This could include work products, e-mails, personal letters, and instant messaging chats. This also can include all usernames, user identifications, and passwords entered during this time, which grants the attacker even more access to the victim's life. These user accounts could be for online banking, travel arrangements, personal dating sites, or any other Web site the victim visits. To complicate matters, these keystroke loggers can easily be delivered to the thief's computer through spyware, Trojan horses, and adware, which he can pick up during a Web site visit or when he installs a particular piece of software.

A relatively new service available on the Internet is a dangerous piece of technology used in conjunction with voice over internet protocol (VOIP) phone systems. VOIP phone systems are becoming very popular with large business today because of their ability to leverage the existing data network infrastructure and transmit phone call traffic over the Internet instead of the normal phone switch from the phone company. Figure 5-1 illustrates a screenshot from Spoofcard.com, which allows a user to connect through this Web site and contact a person using this technology. If you review this service closely, you will see this site allows the user the option to spoof[‡] their caller identification that is displayed and even change their voice so they cannot be identified by the call receiver. Although privacy advocates might herald these kinds of tools, they can be dangerous if used maliciously and may present new challenges for security professionals dealing with harassment or stalking in the workplace.

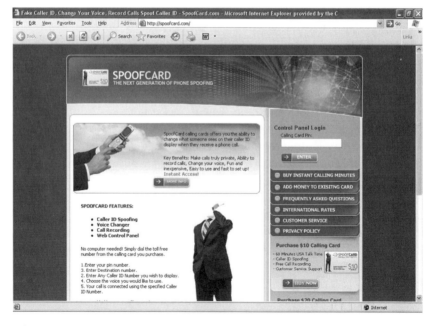

**Figure 5-1** Spoof card.

---

[‡]Spoof: Change the caller ID so it reads something that is incorrect.

The use of "phishing"§ in the propagation of online fraud has literally exploded over the past few years, costing businesses and individuals billions of dollars. Phishing uses known holes in your Internet browser to enable you to be redirected to an illegitimate web site when you click on a falsely identified Web link embedded in an unsolicited e-mail.

The even worse news is that it gets easier almost every day to perpetrate these activities. Consider Figure 5-2, which pertains to "pod slurping." This nasty little practice essentially enables employees to bring their iPods or similar devices to work and, while appearing to be listening to music, they can covertly transfer information off of the computer network and onto their iPod .

These changing security threats are unlikely to decrease in pace or impact. Security practitioners have to work together in the

**Figure 5-2** Pod slurping. (Sturgeon, W. [2005]. Beware the 'pod slurping' employee. Available from: http://news.com.com/ Beware+the+pod+slurping+employee/2100-1029_3-6039926.html. Accessed May 1, 2006.)

---

§Phishing: Using social engineering to inappropriately gain access to personal information.

identification and mitigation of risk, deployment of cogent, holistic security awareness and education programs, and robust investigation methodologies. By building integrated security programs and institutionalizing them across the stakeholder community, practitioners can begin to match the pace of change.

## SECURITY GOVERNANCE STRUCTURES

Depending on the size of your organization, there may be many security governance structures employed, all of which can work. A current common and growing trend is the appointment of a single leader to lead the security risk function. This person, often referred to as the Chief Security Officer (CSO), generally leads both the traditional physical security process as well as today's more common IT security process. This type of structure is often most effective where the IT security role has more of an arm's-length relationship with IT, and the IT security staff is acting as a policy development, audit, or compliance unit rather than an operational unit. Figure 5-3 depicts such a structure.

Another popular governance style today is the use of a Chief Information Security Officer (CISO), a more traditional IT security role that also may have responsibility for physical security. This structure is more commonly used when there is a closer relationship between IT and IT security, or if the company is highly IT-centric. Both these structures can have responsibility for other functions, such as business continuity, emergency management, compliance, employee health and safety, and internal audit (Figure 5-4).

For organizations that have robust, heterogeneous security groups and are trying to approach security enterprise risk management, a "two leaders" format can work, but the governance process and open and honest communication must be strongly

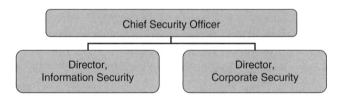

**Figure 5-3**    A common CSO reporting structure.

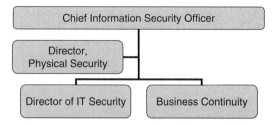

**Figure 5-4** A CISO reporting structure.

entrenched in this approach to be successful. This is especially common in organizations where the two leaders are subject matter experts in their respective disciplines, but each has limited understanding about the technical matters of the other group. This is also common in organizations where security reports at a lower level in the common structure and has yet to gain significant relevance or recognition. Figure 5-5 depicts a two leaders format.

Probably one of the most common security governance structures today is the use of risk councils. Risk councils are committees that regularly meet to discuss all security, occupational health and safety (OH&S), or other risk management issues. These groups can be excellent teams to proactively address the identification, assessment, and mitigation of enterprise-wide risk. These groups are also great at evangelizing the risk messages consistently across the organization; otherwise, you can have too many people enunciating the same message at different entry points to senior management and staff (Figure 5-6).

**Figure 5-5** Emerging two leaders format.

**Figure 5-6**    Risk council activities.

# 6

# *Changing the Business Model*

To understand why convergence has become an organizational imperative, we must first track how the business model has migrated from being primarily geographically isolated entities trading with customers within the reaches of a nation's infrastructure, to electronic marketplaces with no physical addresses or bricks-and-mortar storefronts.

Initially, the security challenge for a businesses was to defend its perimeter; fence lines and door locks were the tools of the trade, along with night watchmen with their trusty flashlights. Even international conglomerates with a presence on multiple continents were often organized more like discrete geographical organizations that distribute their products in separate markets. Although they faced similar challenges, they approached their security problems in their own ways. Often, the level of sophistication in criminal activities that organizations faced was seemingly on a par with the maturity of the organization. In this environment, there were many knowledgeable specialists who understood the process throughout the business life cycle, and information was abundant and reasonably clear about how assets could be protected.

The layoffs and massive downsizing of the 1980s seemed to engender cultural change in organizations. Long gone were the days of lifelong employment, and employees were bombarded with changing expectations about how to prepare not just for changing employers, but also changing careers. The global village became a reality and regional economics and outsourcing began to be utilized as financial tools to pressure unions and reduce operating costs.

This new employment era seemed to create an environment where employees' loyalty to the organization was less valued, and this was rewarded by an increase in white-collar crime. Gone were the days when stealing White-Out and pencils was the largest concern; employees with dislocated loyalty began to exploit internal control weaknesses and take advantage of silos in security systems to steal from their employers. As the warehouse and the order desk learned to work together, simple internal fraud began and was proliferated across the world. Now accountants and security people had to begin working together to uncover more complex crimes within the organization.

The global village and the use of outsourced manpower begat the reality of borderless businesses, where distribution channel management became the word of the day and just-in-time supply chain systems increased the velocity of goods transferred and the speed of business. Organizations could now increase production and store fewer raw materials. As this change occurred, so did the complexity of running this type of enterprise. No one person had knowledge of the entire value chain of the organization. Distribution became a science and an industry unto itself; as cross-border transshipment complexity increased, so did the opportunity for loss events. Departmental experts were required to manage these departments and electronic systems were used to track assets throughout the world. Electronic data interchanges (EDIs) were put in place to connect suppliers and customers in the same system, again to speed up product delivery and information access. The security practitioner was now trying to manage risks across continents in real time. The need for physical tools to actually see assets in different parts of the world led to the innovation of introducing CCTV technology to the corporate data network and the Internet.

With these tools and others, security practitioners now try to keep up with the expanding threat paradigm.

At this point, security practitioners have a knowledge gap in understanding the threats the organization faces as fraud begins to occur in electronic programs. Records are changed and assets disappear, all inside the computer. As electronic enterprise expands and companies begin to leverage their electronic assets to communicate with customers in a completely virtual manner through e-business, their assets begin to change. Information is now traded online without a product ever being moved through the traditional supply chain. A firm can be doing business entirely without the traditional security practitioner being able to point a camera at any part of the transaction. This is a huge paradigm shift, as technology practitioners transition into being IT security specialists and begin to conduct security activities in the virtual world.

Such an electronic enterprise can soon draw a massive increase in attacks from online hackers and others, and this creates a level of fear in the customer base that doing business in this manner is not as safe as shopping in stores. In late 1999 and early 2000, after the Y2K hype, we saw the Internet bubble burst and much of the e-business environment collapse. This created a much more integrated business model, where technology is leveraged to become more efficient and most businesses develop both an online and a bricks-and-mortar delivery channel. The physical security community leverages this technology as well, and moves most of the formal, stand-alone security systems to network-enabled devices, thus leaving the traditional security professionals in a situation where they operate their systems but do not actually understand how they work.

As before, as this new level of complexity is created, a new threat from within is enabled. There are now highly complex business and security systems operating inside organizations, with distinct security functions existing in the management of physical and IT threats and risks. The threats an organization faces are themselves complex and often nondiscrete, with the losses characterized by both traditional and IT security elements. The reality is that security is a weakest-link discipline and no one approach can mitigate all business risks.

The creation of the electronic marketplace, such as eBay.com or Amazon.com, presented an interesting challenge. Because these businesses have limited physical assets, protecting the availability of their electronic assets has become a serious business priority. Maintaining the availability of electronic systems is very much about the physical protection of those assets, and here we see a need to physically protect the electronics by using new methods. The creation of commercial "server farms" and computer bunker facilities creates high-security spaces where physical access control is highly valued. Here we see the beginning of serious business continuity planning in the electronic world, where physical and IT security practitioners must work together for the benefit of the organization. With the advent of recent terrorist attacks in North America, Asia, and Europe, businesses have learned that physical security of assets could have serious impacts on their ability to continue serving customers.

Both the physical security and IT security industries have ramped up to develop high-tech solutions to the security risks their customers face. Two problems exist here. The first is that these systems often duplicate functionality and this can lead to superfluous costs being incurred by firms because they do not have sufficient in-house expertise to integrate both the IT and physical systems. The second problem is that gaps can occur between siloed security systems, and these gaps are exploited by criminals or people with internal knowledge of the organization. For example, in many organizations it is unclear who is responsible for proactively securing the telephone system from fraud and misuse, or who is responsible for ensuring that wiring and maintenance closets are not penetrated and building systems accessed.

The changing business model, as described to this point, has presented security practitioners with an ever-changing business environment in which to assess risk and protect assets. The introduction of new, more technically oriented security practitioners creates a communication need for practitioners on both sides to learn about each other's methods, and how to communicate, and how best to protect the organization. Given the continuing pace of change in business and the ever-increasing complexity of business systems, the business model itself will no doubt be a serious factor in determining which mechanisms and processes are used to defend the business environment.

# 7

# *The Ever-Advancing Microchip*

If you have ever wondered why security is converging, all you have to do is look at the innovation and performance advantages of the ever-advancing microchip. Until newer disruptive technologies come along, this will be the mainstay of computer processing. Much of the world around us advances at the pace of change in microchips. These microchips are found in computers, cars, appliances, transportation systems, and many more devices we use in daily life. The efficiency and effectiveness of these technologies, and the pace at which they change, can be tracked and the future pace of change can be projected.

To start with, let us look at Moore's Law. In 1965, Graham Moore, cofounder of Intel, made a prediction that the number of transistors that could fit into a given space would double every two years. This translates into computing power and was an enormous prediction, but it has held true since then. In 1965, according to the Intel web site, "[O]ne transistor was worth approximately 1 dollar; by 1975 it was worth less than a penny. Intel made a strategic decision to facilitate the convergence of platforms including computing and communications."[1]

The second part of this prediction was that the cost of this increasing computing power would decrease while the performance increased. Here we have the primordial stages of the enabling events that would drive the creation of the new electronic security industry.

The creation of the modern network has enabled physical security controls to be built on technology platforms, delivering increased speed, centralized control, and enhanced security. It also was the beginning of the fracturing of the traditional security professional's job description. Security professionals who did not have backgrounds in electronics and computing were now being inundated with new technologies they did not understand, and the cost and time of learning were prohibitive. Engineers in labs were designing new technologies and security specialists began to emerge. Although I cannot pinpoint the exact date, I submit that this is when convergence began.

Another interesting law to consider is Metcalfe's Law. Robert Metcalfe, the founder of 3M, posited that the value of an organization's network increases exponentially with the number of nodes (or devices) on it. Now this may be difficult to prove to the penny, but the concept holds up fairly well. The interesting part is that, until some years ago, the corporate security department was responsible for protecting expensive assets such as inventory, information in file cabinets, and intellectual property. Now, in this virtual world we live in, much of an organization's worth can exist only in electronic form, where corporate security has limited involvement in many organizations.

The impact on security technology and the tools security practitioners use to secure an organization's assets has been astounding. Whereas the industry used to build stand-alone infrastructures so that clients could run their security products on proprietary systems that were large, bulky, and divisive, now many security systems are fully integrated into the overall network architecture, utilizing the same operating system as desktop users.

The ability to integrate the traditional physical security systems (such as access control and CCTV) into the company data network allows the organization to take advantage of economies of scale, and to leverage the existing infrastructure to deliver many benefits to the organization. These benefits can include utilizing the existing transmission medium (such as the corporate data network), which reduces costs and increases reliability. It further allows for the sharing of system backup and business continuity resources that reduce duplication and increase system availability. It has centralized incident response programs, which can lead to increased uptime and faster identification of the causes of business interruption or outside attacks. Finally, it leverages purchasing power in the acquisition of common hardware and software systems, which reduces overall IT costs and standardizes equipment for maintenance purposes.

There are impacts of integrating physical security systems and the IT network, and it is safe to say that they are not always fully understood by the organization. Introducing any new technical system into a data network has risk and creates impacts on data flow and resource use. An access control system can contain highly important information and must remain unaltered and secure, while maintaining a high rate of availability.

When introducing traditional physical security systems such as access control and CCTV into the data network, a combination of risks can be inherently accepted by the organization. There are risks to physical security systems from the data network, and issues concerning the data network from the physical security systems placed on them. Generally, these systems are both at greater risk each day because security systems are continuously being interconnected, and this exposes them to new and unknown risks. Further, challenges in deploying systems in a more security-focused manner are contested by the need for speed, cost-effectiveness, and functionality. Finally, the burden of auditing these systems can be difficult and labor-intensive, so auditing often rates a lower priority in the sustainment phase of a project. Let us start by examining the generally shared risks of bringing these two systems together.

The physical security systems often do not use technology as sophisticated as that of the data network, and may in themselves be open to attack or require extra work to secure because they use nonstandard operating systems or databases. Many proprietary technologies in the physical security world must be serviced by the vendor or manufacturer, so this creates a situation where organizations must have untrusted people working on their networks to maintain their systems. Further, they are unable to take advantage of enterprise network technologies, such as patch management, storage, and backup systems. It is quite common for these physical security systems to be maintained by people other than the IT group; typically, it is the *physical* security vendor, who may not maintain the equipment on a time schedule, that offers the optimum level of protection. For example, access control vendors may sell a system to an organization with a maintenance agreement to maintain the server on which the application runs. However, if that agreement is not renewed or some functions in the organization are outsourced, these patching and maintenance services might not be completed, thereby exposing the systems to compromise through viruses or other malicious activities. This can impact the network because a compromised computer or server can be used to attack the rest of the network and, even though IT may have protected their systems, they can come under attack through these other systems they do not control.

Another challenge physical security systems can face is that the physical security department might not always be in control of, or even informed of, what IT is doing on the network and they can be impacted by activities such as patching, virus scanning, ports and services allowed, and third parties with network access. This shared level of risk between these groups and systems should be ample evidence that cooperation between departments is paramount, given the evolution of technology and the microchip.[§]

## QUANTUM COMPUTING[‡]

Much of our security infrastructure, both physical and IT, is built on the assumption that by assessing the risk and applying the appropriate security controls, our assets will be more or less safe. We can make complex user IDs and passwords, secret codes, and even use complex encryption methods that are unbreakable with today's mainstream technology. Yet the security practitioner must remain vigilant and not be seduced by a single-point solution because, although the microchip may have its benefits in protecting you, it also has limitations.

---

[§]For more on this, see the Alliance for Enterprise Security Risk Management (AESRM) study titled "Convergent Security Risks in Physical Security Systems and IT Infrastructures." Available from: http://www.aesrm.org/Convergent%20Sec%20Risks %20Physical%20Sec%20Systems.pdf.
[‡]The author is not an expert in quantum computing, but this section is based on reading from the Centre for Quantum Computing Web site and related articles. Available from: www.qubit.org.

Quantum computing is a new field of study that uses quantum mechanics to enable computers to process information–in a new and radically more efficient way. Now, without getting into the exciting world of quantum mechanics, this effectively means that computers can compute multiple calculations simultaneously instead of in a series. To put this into practice, imagine these two scenarios:

1.  Trying to enter the alarm codes to an intrusion alarm system.
    With existing technology, using the "brute force" attack to determine the correct code to enter into an alarm system, you have to try each one in series until you find a code that works. With quantum computing, the computer would be able to try every conceivable code combination simultaneously.

2.  Cracking strong encryption.
    One of the strengths of public key encryption (PKE) is that to crack the private key that the data owner holds can take a very long time, and this is a major deterrent to trying. Some encryption algorithms are so complex that it could take a user's entire lifetime to have a computer try all the possible combinations to crack an encryption code. Again, with a quantum calculation this could be done simultaneously to dramatically speed up the process. This presents a serious problem because encryption is the tool we use to protect really important matters such as national secrets, our financial resources, and military launch codes.

This presents significant opportunities for the brute force attack to have a significant impact on the world of security should quantum computing become an actual commercial tool, not just the theoretical area of study that it is today.[†]

## REFERENCE

1.  Hiremane, R. From Moore's law to Intel innovation–Prediction to reality. Available from: www.intel.com/technology/magazine/silicon/moores-law-0405.htm. Accessed August 27, 2005.

---

[†]For a more detailed discussion on how quantum computing can impact encryption, please review the discussion paper by Artur Ekert at www.qubit.org/library/intros/cryptana.html#node1.

# Leveraging Technology

## 8

Given advancing technology and the operations of business, there are many implications for security professionals, including benefits to management ability, cost competitiveness, and even strategic positioning for the enterprise. Advancements in technology allow the security professional to manage a larger staff and geographical area; the global village facilitates a lower price point on manpower and technology; and the importance of security in this post-9/11 and e-business bubble-bursting world allows security-conscious organizations to attract and retain customer market share.

One of the challenges most managers have had to deal with over the past 20 years is an increasing "span of control,"[1] or the number of direct reports they must directly supervise. According to Wikipedia,

> In the hierarchical business organization of the past it was not uncommon to see average spans of 1 to 10 or even less. That is, one manager supervises ten employees on average. In the 1980s there was a flattening of organizational structures causing average spans to move closer to 1 to 100. This was made possible by the introduction of inexpensive information technology that replaced many middle managers (whose main task had been to

collect information from operational managers, compile it, and present it to upper management). Computers also made feasible the task of managing larger groups.[2]

Security professionals can now have a larger span of control that includes multiple offices on numerous continents, controlled right from their desktops. Web space work groups, wherein teams virtually meet for conferences and regular team meetings, cross boundaries of geography. With the advancement of web camera technology, meeting participants can see each other in the web meeting space. Utilizing CCTV over the corporate data network, managers can operate surveillance cameras anywhere in the world from their desktops. Global organizations can link one access control system through their own data network, across countries and continents. The ability to leverage technology has given managers the tools to effectively manage larger teams; if done well, this can positively impact cost and cohesiveness.

Although not a completely new concept, security technology can be a service to business groups. Line of business managers can use surveillance systems to monitor employee performance or safety conditions in the workplace. Information sharing can lead to much organizational efficiency, including increased profit and effective use of resources.

Correlating people-counting systems that track the number of customers who enter a mall with the incident data tracked in the security incident tracking system can inform security management about when the most likely traffic trends necessitate extra staff to be assigned to patrol the facility, and when fewer resources may be an acceptable risk. In one organization I worked for, we moved one guard from the night shift because incidents were low during that time, and stationed him on the afternoon shift when incident traffic was higher. We added an intrusion alarm to the facility and supplemented the night shift with occasional mobile patrols of the site. This translated into an annual savings of more than $100,000 and provided more security coverage when it was needed—during high-incident periods.

## VELOCITY OF RECOVERY

Employing network infrastructure and allowing IT professionals to manage the physical security systems can leverage the traditionally superior uptime and availability of the data network and can allow security technology to benefit from this reliability. The interconnectivity of technology systems has meant that when one system becomes unavailable or goes down, other connected systems can suffer the same fate. In the context of security systems, the movement to enterprise security platforms, which manage alarms, handle access control, and provide CCTV monitoring all in one system, has increased the necessity to provide a high level of assurance that these systems will be available on a 24/7 basis. This business need can only be met by either building a fully redundant security infrastructure or leveraging the existing IT infrastructure to provide the redundancy.

The backup and recovery capabilities common to the IT data networks of larger organizations provide a high level of assurance for risk-facing departments and can be used to provide this assurance for traditional security systems. This involves the security systems being connected to technology such as patch management, network performance monitoring, and business continuity systems. Patch management systems ensure that computers are continually updated with critical fixes for security holes identified in their software. System monitoring tools can manage uptime through identifying and categorizing system performance of the hardware that runs the security applications. Business continuity systems, such as redundant servers, backup systems, hot sites, and snapshot systems, allow the organization to quickly recover from service interruption or physical disasters.

The ability to be more reliable and therefore more secure than your competitors can even lead to a firm gaining a robust, strategic, competitive advantage in their industry. For more on this, see Chapter 18 on strategic differentiation.

After 9/11, many firms were left without electronic systems, Internet access, and other technologies. The firms that responded to help first were no doubt those that had robust continuity strategies and, very likely (although this was probably not their motivation), they gained business in the aftereffect by assessing their customers' future needs for service upon rebuilding their businesses.

The concept of the global village, or the shrinking of the world's business and social community through technology and transportation, has had a significant effect on corporations' abilities to lower incremental costs of business through transferring of labor-intensive functions to jurisdictions that have a relatively lower price point for workers. One such example is a service whereby organizations with large numbers of CCTV cameras to be monitored can transfer the monitoring function to places such as Bangalore, India. Bangalore, well-known as a region to which technology functions such as call centers have been outsourced, can provide services such as monitoring CCTV systems across the Internet for a very competitive cost. Organizations can drive down the price point of these necessary services because the cost of labor in that location is lower than in many other jurisdictions.

Some of the complaints related to the outsourcing of call centers have been related to communication skills and accents of the locals providing the service. However, with video monitoring this struggle is not nearly as intense. Given that communication only needs to happen when a report is necessary, the majority of such service is provided without cultural implications. Although I am not suggesting that outsourcing either is or is not the appropriate course of action, it is important to recognize the ability to leverage the technology—a combination of the Internet and the CCTV system—to lower costs, maintain reliability, and potentially gain competitive advantage. This example does not address the potential risks of this choice, but it is an example of the use of technology as a business enabler.

No discussion of leveraging technology would be complete without acknowledging that there are inherent risks associated with leveraging technology. Technology tends to be commonly acquired because it is "cool" or nice to have. This is a very dangerous scenario, because technology needs to be managed and maintained, and any systems not maintained can become a security risk for the environment. Remote computing (the ability for business people to connect to systems while away from their business environment) is incredibly valuable and is, in itself, a competitive advantage over businesses without this ability. The velocity of transactions and customer contact and the ability to complete work while away from the office is incredibly valuable. But this ability comes at a price and that price is security risk, which without proper management can represent a huge security risk to the organization. Wireless and VOIP technologies are other higher-risk technologies that business often wants to take advantage of. It is important that security professionals be vigilant in assessing the risks associated with all technologies employed by their organizations, and recognize that, on the surface, technology can represent a great advantage to the business, but that "the devil is always in the details" when it comes to the security issues in all technologies.

## REFERENCES

1.  Robbins, S.P. (1999). Span of control. In: Essentials of Organizational Behaviour, 6th edition. Upper Saddle River, NJ: Prentice Hall, p. 14.
2.  Wikipedia Web site. Span of control. Available from: http://en.wikipedia.org/wiki/Span_of_control. Accessed August 27, 2006.

# *The New World*

# 9

# *Disruptive Technology and Other Stuff*

In order to understand the new world that security professionals face, it is prudent to understand the drivers that have enabled or contributed to the convergence of the risks and threats their organizations face. The basic premise of convergence is that security must be employed in a new, more integrated way. Part of the challenge of making this case is helping all parties understand how and why the business ecosphere has changed. Let us first look at some of these key components of the changing world for security professionals.

## ACCESS TO INFORMATION IS EASIER

Information is published either legitimately or illegitimately, easily and quickly, 24 hours a day, around the world. Evidence or assets can be digitized and converted to Web content, and e-mailed or faxed in a matter of moments. A crime or loss of proprietary information can occur across multiple jurisdictions with limited ability of the owner to recover the loss.

## MASSIVE DISTRIBUTION AND A GLOBAL FOOTPRINT

Organizations have decentralized assets from safe and secure legacy locations, and have spread them across the world. Manufacturing plants or outsourced services can be located in remote jurisdictions where security controls are less reliable or risk profiles are more hostile. Many countries where businesses operate have different legal and business rules that impact an organization's ability to protect itself. In some countries the legal concept of "privilege" is not recognized, so lawyers being deposed by opposing counsel in a legal proceeding can be compelled to reveal discussions between their clients and themselves. Some countries do not recognize the rights of businesses to their exclusive use of their intellectual property or will not cooperate in the owners' legitimate protection attempts. The movement of online music sharing and gambling to offshore locations, beyond the reach of domestic laws, presents difficulties for those wishing to engage them. Given the combination of the global reach of the Internet and World Wide Web, and the exponential distribution power of servers and software, businesses have major challenges in dealing with foreign or remote risks that face them. This global distribution ability is only more deadly when combined with mechanized or automated threats.

## ABILITY TO AUTOMATE ATTACKS

The risks and difficulties facing the safe cracker, cat burglar, or common thief who tries to break into a building are fairly well understood. The attack is generally a balance between brute force and skill, depending on the target and the finesse of the assailant. Unfortunately, the cyber world is much more mystical, and fewer people have the capabilities to crack the online or internal assets of an organization. Further, the protections and threats are generally understood by few in the organization. Also, technology allows for attacks to be automated in such a way that the attacker need not be near the asset at all. Compare the bank robber of old who had to drive by the bank and drop off his accomplices, versus a robot that continually tries to break into the bank all night without the robber being nearby—at no risk from law enforcement. Then, if the robot gets in, the robber need only give the robot some further instruction to begin the process of trying to crack the safe. All the while, the robber is sipping cappuccino down at the local Starbucks. This is, in effect, the new world we live in: automated attacks by robot programs that search the Internet or internal servers for vulnerable targets 24 hours a day, and they are a serious threat. If you manage a database of customer information, financial data, or your company's access control system, this should be of concern. Now imagine if all the safes in all the offices were connected somehow!

## INTERCONNECTIVITY OF DEVICES

To improve the effectiveness and efficiency of organizations and the productivity of staff, computer systems have been linked together in ways never before seen. With authentication and access control mechanisms such as single sign-on and directory services, many of the organization's assets can be made available without having to go through the challenge response (user ID and password) process at each asset. Although this speeds up the process for staff and visitors accessing data, it also creates an "all the eggs in one basket" scenario that puts a tremendous strain on the security of the credentials being used for authentication. If, when entering the building, a staff member or visitor only had to show identification once and then they were granted access to everything in the facility, one might suggest that it is a little too easy to get around. This trade-off between convenience (or functionality, in the IT world) and security creates a decision that needs to be made over and over for the security professional and the organization. How much security is enough?

For discussion, see the security continuum in Figure 9-1. The security continuum represents the concept that true security and functionality are actually juxtaposed. Most organizations pick their location on the continuum. It is an individual position based on risk tolerance and resources, or lack of information and awareness. This may be the decision to secure a building with a door lock or an access control system, or the decision to require a password on a web application; it is a decision about how much security is appropriate. Each security decision point on the diagram in Figure 9-1 represents a security decision and the risk and functionality that the decision delivers. These do not have to be decisions that are made;

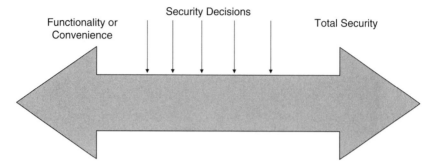

**Figure 9-1** The security continuum.

they can just as easily be the evasion of a decision. By choosing to not make a decision or to avoid a situation, a location on the continuum is chosen because a set of controls exists, somewhere between no controls and complete control.

So, given the movement to interconnect physical and IT devices, the pressure is increased to make prudent security decisions. By creating this interconnectivity, the organization is moved farther to the left along the axis. This makes it easier for users to connect and access resources and assets. In doing so, there is a price to be paid in terms of security. In effect, ease of use creates security weaknesses, whereas a stronger security posture generally reduces functionality of user overhead and administration.

Look at Microsoft Windows products: most are really easy to use and are useful for most people. That is great, but for many years Microsoft *enjoyed* its products' reputation of being inherently insecure. This reputation primarily comes from their having been apparently designed for ease of use. Many of the other software operating systems that boasted about being more secure, such as Unix or Macintosh, were also harder to use or less easy to work with across an enterprise. The short answer here is that, in general, the easier it is to access something, the less secure it is likely to be. This is not really rocket science, but it is important when we talk about the new risks associated with interconnectivity of business assets across technology platforms and worldwide geographies.

This interconnectivity risk is only worsened when you consider the relatively low number of protocols‡ and transmission mediums we use to transmit electronic information.

## MASSIVE RELIANCE ON HOMOGENEOUS PROTOCOLS

When you think about it, we do not actually rely on many distinct systems for most of our communication. These days, almost anything can run over the Internet: computer data, e-mail, video, Internet chat and instant messaging, and even Internet telephone. We can do our banking and shopping, communicate socially and for business, and even maintain personal relationships of one form or another, all over the TCP/IP§-based Internet.

The other major communication protocol we use is the traditional telephone. One could argue there are two different protocols with the telephone, given that some are digital and some are analog, but to the uninitiated I will call this one protocol for the sake of the discussion. The fax machine is also a telephone-based protocol that operates over the telephone system in a similar manner to the telephone.

The point here is that attackers who want to attack the primary communication mediums of business, do not have to master too many technologies before they learn how to exploit them for profit and malicious satisfaction. In another example, imagine you were a miscreant who wanted to destabilize the auto industry, causing panic in the buying community by introducing flaws into the designs and engineering of different lines of cars. The choices are literally massive as to where to start. There are dozens of lines of vehicles and hundreds of models, so to affect the entire industry would seem very difficult. Now consider impacting the sum total of electronic commerce on the Internet. Before Y2K, most businesses were rushing to get a Web presence on the Internet and begin doing electronic commerce. Businesses spent millions of dollars to become ready to capture the Internet customer. However,

---

‡Protocol: A set of instructions for computer systems to follow to talk to each other and transmit data between them.
§TCP/IP: Transmission control protocol/Internet protocol. Protocol to aid in transmitting data across the Internet.

when the Internet bubble burst, it was in part because the online consumer had a low level of confidence that they were safe doing business online. Previously, very public online breaches of customer credit card and personal data had exposed a costly secret: the Internet was designed for ease of use and functionality, but not for security. As we discussed this concept earlier in the chapter with the security continuum, functionality comes at the expense of security. This reliance on these limited protocols makes it easy for attackers to garner a high level of knowledge and expertise in exploiting this one technology.

## VERY FEW END-TO-END SECURITY SOLUTIONS

The creation of independent security silos and technology has often limited vendors to developing single-point solutions. This is also common because technology was especially complex in the early days and connecting proprietary protocols together was not always possible. This leaves many security professionals in the situation of not having an end-to-end security solution and having to manage multiple systems, gather risk and threat data output from many sources, and manually combine it to conduct analysis. One of the challenges of endeavoring to make disparate systems work together is that often the system weaknesses are in deployment and configuration of the independent systems or the interfaces between the systems. More firms are now beginning to either make their own full-service systems or combine compatible technologies and support them as one solution.

## HISTORICAL MEASUREMENTS OF BUSINESS SUCCESS ARE BASED ON QUARTERLY PROFIT AND REVENUE

Any security professional would agree that security is not usually a function that can be measured on a quarterly basis. Although I am not saying that we cannot measure activity-based incidents quarterly, I do believe the success of a security program is best measured over years of experience dealing with annual cyclical events, budget cycles, and seasonal or regional challenges. Business often tends to allocate resources and compensate leaders based on quarterly profits and financial impacts. Limited "business value-protected" or "risk-mitigated" metrics exist on the performance measures of the business, and this is one of the issues impacted when security projects get done. If we could demonstrate how security directly enabled those quarterly profits and revenues, security might be seen in a more favorable light, not as a cost center. For more on this, please see Chapter 24, The Case for Security and Convergence.

## THE NEED TO FEED THE BEAST

The never-ending desire to feed the beast has made the medium become the threat. The theoretical beast in this example is the public's and businesses' desire for more services. Consumer demand for more, better, and faster online, real-time, 24/7 bandwidth, pornography, video clips, news, entertainment, Web content, VOIP, and blogs has driven the industry to create more communication and enabling mechanisms for people to easily, and insecurely, communicate and be entertained. All this technology, desire for ease of use, and push for consumerism has driven the business ecosphere to become a dangerous place to operate in and a difficult place to secure.

# 10

## *The Need for Education*

Let us start this discussion from the premise that we all agree that security is a weakest-link discipline. So we can agree that having 75% of your security locked up tight still leaves another 25% of the organization vulnerable. This seems quite logical, but this is much of what the argument for convergence is about and aims to resolve. It is often the weakest-link security controls in the organization where exploitation is prone to happen. The receptionist who leaves her network password taped to her computer monitor or under her keyboard potentially defeats the $500,000 investment the organization has in the firewall, access control list, and other security mechanisms.

To cut to the chase here, doing full convergence requires understanding, knowledge, and perspective. Understanding is required because the process of integrating security organizations may be a rocky journey with many challenges and roadblocks along the way; knowledge is necessary because determining the aspects of convergence that will work for your organization is crucial for the starting points towards initial success; and perspective is important because at least one person needs to stand back and view the overall, enterprise-wide progress in the company's security posture and adjust the plan as necessary to enable convergence to be as relevant as possible. As mentioned earlier, convergence is not a roadmap per se, but a framework for success that requires creativity and leadership.

Security practitioners attempting convergence need to have, at the bare minimum, an appreciation for all of the aspects of security risk in the organization. They will get this through a combination of events. The first event is the garnering of education and professional development opportunities to ensure that the security team can at least speak the language of all the security risk-facing functions in the organization. The second event is reviewing the security posture of the organization with wide-open eyes to absorb all the potential risk they previously did not fully appreciate. Finally, they must examine—in detail, with the other security practitioners—the enterprise security risks that exist in their organization and begin to own all of these issues for themselves. The old attitude that a security risk is not in their department is difficult to substantiate in this new post–paradigm-shift world.

Given that most of the security threats that organizations face today have converged in some way, a holistic approach to these security issues will be beneficial for any security program. I have seen no indicators that suggest a slowing of the pace in the technological revolution or the pace of integration of security threats that organizations are facing. Security practitioners who have a post–World War II and pre-Internet world mindset will undoubtedly feel their sphere of expertise closing in on them. That is to say, being a physical security or IT security specialist will soon not be sufficient to be a relevant and fully informed professional. Forward-looking practitioners—even those without any crossover skills—will surely begin to understand that they cannot do the job properly unless they understand all the security risks their organization faces. The simple reality is that the more applied knowledge you have about the security risks and the posture of your organization, the less risk your organization is likely to face.

If you are closing in on retirement and have the luxury of avoiding this new world of threats, count yourself lucky. The rest of us who still have at least 10 years or more left in our careers must begin to have an enterprise-wide appreciation of all -

security threats or we risk being left behind professionally. It has always been said that information is power and I do not believe for a second that learning something new is easy. Even though mediocrity is easy, forcing yourself and your organization to seek excellence in security risk mitigation is difficult, but worth the effort, given the risks that face the organization.

One of the roadblocks in learning something new is fear, so learning about the other side of the industry may seem daunting at first. However, as someone who has made the journey, I assure you any serious security professional can make it if they have the willingness to try.

If you are an IT security practitioner, it is essential to understand why you should care about physical security and how you can begin to learn about what security professionals do. To start with, it is important to understand their function because they are integrating more and more technology onto the corporate data network every year, and with this equipment comes new risk for the network environment and the data you are so judiciously trying to protect. Further, given the growth of one-card or smart-card authentication and access control platforms, it is almost a certainty that this integration challenge will face you at some point in the future. Recall my words from earlier chapters about third-party vendors supplying systems to the physical security department that may go unsupported after a period of time; consider what these risks look like for the network and the organization. Consider that CCTV technologies are moving from encoded analog systems to full digital, IP addressable devices that will be hogging network bandwidth if not properly deployed and managed. Further, consider the opportunities to merge these technologies with existing IT storage systems, such as patch management or the corporate storage area network (SAN). Also, realize that investigations are becoming more integrated on an evolving basis and the level of cooperation between your two groups will need to evolve along with it.

When starting simple conversations with your physical security colleagues, it is best to speak to them in English rather than in techie jargon or acronym-speak. Terms such as VPN, IP, IDS, NAT, or DoS are not appropriate to use in conversation when trying to build a bridge between groups. Although you may understand how relatively simple these acronyms are in the IT security world, they are foreign to the traditional physical security practitioner and may build fear and doubt in the person you are addressing. This is not a sermon from an academic; I speak from personal experience, both as someone who has had to learn this terminology and as a practitioner who now has to explain it to others. Try speaking in terms of security perimeters or by relating the value of a database in terms of the risk of exposure of this asset; or try likening the risk issues to real-world examples instead of to the technical realities of the risks. You are communicating effectively if you can answer one question: Was my aim in the conversation to educate? That is what you must do to communicate well to a nontechnical person.

Consider a simple example when explaining the difference between a desktop computer and a server. A technical explanation of this will include a review of the features of both and what they do, the size of their hard drives, processing power, and other assorted technical information. However, the educator will explain the difference between a desktop computer and the server with real-world analogies. The difference between a desktop and a server is akin to the difference between a car and a bus; both the car and the bus transport people, but one has more horsepower and capacity than the other. The same is true for computers—one can store more information and has more horsepower for performing activities; it is about horsepower and capacity. This simple example starts the conversation with a common base on which to build. This will entice the nontechnical person to want to know more, and in just that moment you will have not only won that person's respect, you will have also become an educator.

Remember that physical security practitioners protect your buildings, people, and assets. You can learn a lot from them, because they are natural risk managers and usually possess a healthy level of paranoia. They can be your allies when discussing risk, especially where people are involved. They can also be your comrades when senior management wants to eviscerate your security budget and you need support in making your argument against such an action.

If you are a physical security practitioner, the need to understand the technology is essential and the serious risks this technology delivers to your organization is undeniable. But, as a place to start, you must first divorce yourself from any thoughts that IT security is too difficult to understand, because it is not. Now I do not want you to think I am suggesting you can be out there configuring firewalls and hacking the network, but you can get the basics. You need these basics to begin to understand the technology risks that face your organization; you need to incorporate these risks into your security awareness and training programs; and you need to communicate these aggregate risks to senior management.

Start by finding an *IT for Dummies* book or approach someone who can explain the basics of how security technology works and impacts your organization. Then, try to translate this in terms of the functions you perform in physical security. The user ID and password you use to log into the computer is just a method to identify and authenticate who you are, similar to an employee badge or a proximity card. A firewall is a perimeter protection device designed to permit access to the company assets by authorized persons and keep out all others; this is not dissimilar at all to a perimeter fence and a staffed gatehouse. Even technical concepts like network intrusion detection systems (IDSs) can become easy to understand when explained correctly. An IDS is a system that monitors activity on the computer network between the perimeter and the assets (the firewall and the computers), looking for action that is suspicious or fits a known pattern of malicious behavior. This might be from a user, a hacker, or from some malicious software, such as a virus. Now let us try this in the real world. The space between the perimeter fence and the building (the perimeter and the assets, as above) is a place that is patrolled by a guard, a dog, a camera—all of these are seeking the same thing, which is to identify inappropriate or suspicious behavior by someone who is in that area.

I hope these explanations are straightforward enough for you to see that these two worlds are not so different and that you, as a physical security practitioner, can easily learn this technology and add value. Given that we know that a high proportion of security breaches are related to the actions of people and not the technology, I will leave you with one example to show you how you can add value and that you probably already possess most of the experience you need to engage in many IT security conversations. Consider your standard physical security access control system that permits users to utilize their employee badges to come and go from company buildings. Then think about how many people are still in that system who should not have access cards; hopefully the answer is zero. If it is not, it is probably because there has been a breakdown in the process somewhere between a company employee or human resources not informing you that a person has left so that you can revoke their privileges. This phenomenon is exactly the same in IT security; remember what I said in Chapter 3 about security personnel being the last to know? Well, IT security is no different. Consider asking your IT security person how confident he or she is that every person in the access control system has the correct privileges. In other words, is it possible there are unauthorized people with access to the network? You will probably see the blood drain from their face or their shoulders slump when they admit they are not sure. They face the same issues you do; start the conversation—the concerns are the same!

# 11

## Cyber Crime: A Pervasive Threat

Although governments have been debating and proposing computer crime legislation as far back as 1977, when Sen. Abe Ribicoff
introduced the Federal Computer Systems Protection Act, cyber
crime legislation has been fractured and disjointed, to say the least.
The challenge of cyber crime is that it is not a simple thing to say
that the "crime" occurred in a specific jurisdiction. Questions that
arise include:

1.  Did the crime occur where the victim is located?
2.  Did it occur where the computer server is located?
3.  What if one act involved multiple crimes committed in
    different jurisdictions?
4.  What if one jurisdiction has more powerful legislation to
    prosecute? Can jurisdiction be transferred?
5.  Can everyone accused be extradited to those other
    jurisdictions?

If you are a corporate security specialist trying to get justice for a staff member who has lost his or her identity because of a malicious incursion into your network, you are faced with an exasperating fact of life.

Since the role of the dedicated IT security professional was created, they have been primarily taking the responsibility for reacting to these types of incidents in the organization. Now that we see the volume of personal information stored in electronic form in our organizations increasing on an exponential scale, along with the interconnected nature of attacks, it is often difficult to say whether an investigation should be handled solely by IT or physical security. The threats have converged, and this leads us to the immutable fact that, in order to properly respond to investigations of cyber crime and crimes against people and their information, our investigation techniques are going to have to converge as well.

Attacks from both the outside and inside of the organization can result in losses of personal information that can be used against employees and customers. The use of "Bot nets," or legions of compromised computers that can be used by an attacker for nefarious purposes, have become one of the primary enabling tools for massive distribution of malicious attacks. When combined, they can be used for many attacks against an organization, such as a "denial of service" attack against your company Web site, firewall, and servers. Now if this firewall is your main access point to the Internet, it may have a devastating effect on communications such as CCTV traffic, VOIP, or mission-critical e-mail.

Recently, new prosecutions have begun to appear in the U.S. courts that show a level of maturing in cyber legislation. In May, 2006, a federal court convicted the first person of profiting from the use of Bot nets. The case was *United States v. Ancheta* in California, and the U.S. district court sentenced Jeanson James Ancheta to 57 months of federal prison time.[1] There are also cases of disgruntled former employees who committed crimes against the technology and assets of their former employers and were held accountable (specifically, *United States v. Cotton* in New York and *United States v. Angle* in Massachusetts).

Comprehensive and binding cyber crime legislation has been signed by a large number of countries. The Council of Europe, with its 46 member states, created new cyber crime legislation in 2001;

Canada, Japan, South Africa, and the United States are additional signatories to the convention.

The introduction of organized crime as a major player in cyber crime has forever changed the stakes for security practitioners dealing with these new threats. When it was only a handful of students in universities around the world releasing viruses and worms to the Internet, organizations could afford to take a laissez-faire attitude toward the economics of the risks, but now with legislation making people potentially criminally accountable for lapses in protective action, cyber crime has an entirely new level of priority.

The economics of cyber crime have made it possible for organized crime to hire skilled professional programmers to design spyware systems to deliver malicious code on a mass scale to enable the collection of personal information sufficient for identity theft. I recently heard a statistic that the average identity theft costs all involved around $50,000! If you can steal and exploit thousands of identities a year, this is a real money-making industry.

The impact on corporate security professionals is that they are currently left in the dark, waiting for IT security or outside forensic consultants to help them discern what occurred with their assets. All these issues are enabled and are escalating by the use and pervasive nature of technology. Every time a new device is connected to the Internet and then to assets, or assets are stored on the device, a new risk is born.

At a 2005 IT security conference in Chicago, a speaker commented on the future threats that are facilitated and enabled by new technology. His example purported that there were 850 million IP nodes[‡] in 2004 and approximately 2.1 billion cell phones with no or limited onboard security, and when these phones become IP addressable under 2.5 and 3 G technologies, the troubles of the Internet will have just tripled. Although this may very well be true to some extent, we will have to see what steps the technology manufacturers take in advance to mitigate this risk.

What corporate security departments should be most concerned with is that the average physical security professional knows very little about these issues at this time, and they are often

---

[‡]IP nodes: Endpoints on the Internet.

the primary organizational security resource that deals with the effects of these technology-based threats. The Internet easily enables crimes against people and organizations.

Now that criminals are more sophisticated in their approach and the resources they are willing to engage to achieve their objectives, security needs to adopt an equally sophisticated approach. IT security has been "dumbed down" to the point where many organizations think a firewall and web browsers that use a secure sockets layer (SSL) provide enough protection. Although some of the technology used in IT and IT security is complex, physical security can certainly help in structuring an approach to managing enterprise security risk.

## REFERENCE

1.   United States Department of Justice Web site. (2006). Computer crime and intellectual property section. Computer crime cases. Available from: www.usdoj.gov/criminal/cybercrime/cccases.html. Accessed May 1, 2006.

# 12

## *How These Groups Can Help Each Other*

So now that we have defined what convergence is, why it has come to be, and have described the challenges that security professionals are now facing, we can begin to explore how these two distinct groups (which came from different backgrounds, cultures, and education) can help each other mitigate risk. Let us start with the basics and ask, What are they are both concerned with? The mantra of the physical security practitioner is to protect people, information, and property, whereas the IT security professional is concerned with protecting the confidentiality, integrity, and availability (CIA) of the organization's data and networks. Essentially, these two missions are neither inconsistent with each other nor mutually exclusive. The physical security goal for the protection of information seeks, in general terms and possibly unknowingly, to ensure the CIA of the information. Given the discussion from the Booze Allen Hamilton (BAH) study in Chapter 2 that data has primarily migrated to the electronic form, this is a signal to security practitioners that there is a shared interest in how information is protected.

The physical security goal of protection of property and assets includes the protection of IT hardware and systems, and building locking systems that control access to server rooms and cabling closets. The IT security goal of protecting CIA data is crucial now, given another BAH point from Chapter 2 about the new protective technologies that exist on the corporate data network. These are mission-critical systems for the physical security group and they must be available and unaltered to be effective. Essentially, the work of these two groups is the same in many respects, and practitioners should examine how security mechanisms are the same and how they are different to begin identifying where the cracks in the security program lie.

Access control is still access control, no matter how you look at this security mechanism. Given the implications of the United States Homeland Security Presidential Directive 12, and the impact to access control for those in, or who do business with, the U.S. federal government, it is easy to support the movement toward a closer relationship between physical and IT security groups. These duplicate infrastructure systems present an excellent cost savings opportunity for organizations with the ability to bring the two systems together and reap the benefits of the lower operating costs.

Authentication—the process of confirming the correctness of the claimed identity—is still the same whether in physical or IT security. Both groups use mechanisms to authenticate authorized personnel. Whether they are user IDs and passwords, PIN codes, biometrics, proximity badges, smart cards, or any other combination of tools, they are all still seeking to authenticate that a user who attempts access to an asset is actually who he or she claims to be.

The process of authorization, or the approval of access to an asset, is still the same for both IT and physical security. The interesting piece in this particular discussion is the number of people involved in making decisions regarding who gets access to what asset, and how that is then revoked. There can be many individuals making decisions about who is permitted access to physical spaces, including to which buildings, floors, specific rooms, and equipment. Also, there is often another set of people deciding who is permitted access to which systems, databases, servers, documents, data, and project information. My experience is that these groups very seldom communicate with one another and compare notes;

more often, there is no comprehensive revocation process to all of these authorizations.

As a consultant with IBM and other organizations, I traveled the world reviewing the physical and IT security of many large organizations in numerous countries. The one issue that was universal with all these organizations was that none of them was 100% sure of who had access to their assets. When asked questions regarding their complete certainty that employees who have voluntarily or involuntarily separated from the organization had returned their building access cards and had their IT privileges revoked, none was prepared to answer in the affirmative. I found this unbelievable until I reviewed the fragmented process by which privileges are authorized and revoked in organizations. This is one of the cracks in most organizations that security can help with, no matter which security group you sit in. Beginning the dialogue with human resources, the security groups, business groups, and other stakeholders can start to close this gap. You can start with an audit of who has access to the network and different key enterprise systems, and compare that list to the authorized employee list. Then review the list of which employees have an access card or keys to buildings and other property.

To add another level of sophistication, you can review who has the authority to decide who is allowed access to what asset. Often, these decisions are somewhat arbitrary, or access has been given out in one fashion for so long that the appropriateness of the access goes unreviewed for many years. I have often found that responsibility for giving access privileges has been delegated to individuals with insufficient understanding of the risks to the asset to make optimal decisions about that access. These goals are only enhanced when you add to your review the access rights of current and former consultants and contractors, and third-party support firms, such as IT vendors, business partners, and outsource service providers.

Another area where these groups can aid each other is in the application of compensating controls. Compensating controls are a less desirable security control mechanism used when the optimal internal control is unavailable or is unable to be implemented. For example, a common internal control is the separation of duties whereby no one person should be able to control the entire process of a financial transaction. This is a fairly standard approach, but in some organizations where there are limited resources, sometimes one person must conduct all aspects of a financial transaction. A compensating control in this situation might be to have the employee sign a company "code of conduct" related to this processing, and then have an accountant perform a regular audit of the financial transactions and even log all electronic activities on the financial system. These compensating controls provide for a "best effort" method of reducing risk when the best possible solution is not available.

A strong tool for security practitioners to utilize is working with their counterparts in the selection and application of compensating controls to best mitigate enterprise security risks. Here is a good example of where this has worked effectively: In 1991, I was working as a site security supervisor where a courthouse complex was part of the responsibility. An ongoing court case involved a gang member who had shot an armored car driver; the gang member made a public statement that he would pay $1 million to anyone who could break him out of jail. Upon entering the control room one day, I found an employee printing out a floor plan document of the jail cell area. Now this could have been a completely innocuous event with no direct link to the trial, but I was not planning on taking any chances. We engaged the IT staff in the organization to help us and, although we could not completely cut off access to the information, we were able to restrict access to some pieces of information and we were able to log all views of the sensitive information. Finally, we made it known that the logging had been turned on and every access to any record was being logged and reviewed. I had not known what I was able to do, but by explaining my problem to IT we were able to work together to implement compensating control mechanisms to reduce the risk.

One of the most obvious opportunities available to security practitioners in organizations is the creation of a unified security voice to staff and management. Security awareness, education and training, and status reports to senior management all offer the opportunity for contact points with stakeholders in order to evangelize a message. The unification of security messages delivers a more complete meaning and helps staff—the ones most likely to be at the instigation end of a security risk in the organization—understand what their responsibility is in securing the organization. A great example of this comes from my own organization, where we meet with all levels of management and supervisors as regularly as possible to communicate the security awareness material important at any given time. Getting on the agendas of these groups can be tough, as we are all busy; but once I am there and on the agenda, I use that time to communicate all the security messages, both IT and physical. When my corporate security manager speaks to groups, he can mention the current IT security concerns within his allotted time. Often this brings up questions that can either be addressed on the spot or followed-up afterwards. This is especially important in larger organizations because you may not be afforded the opportunity to appear before certain stakeholder groups too often, and these opportunities to reduce enterprise risk can have profound effects.

"Social engineering" is perhaps the best example of how the threats an organization faces have converged. Although people have been talking themselves past receptionists and into secure areas for years, the risks to organizations have increased considerably because the attackers have been moving from the physical realm to the anonymous cyber world. The ability of technosocial engineers to garner information from the safety of the Internet or phone system, at least metaphorically, opens a Pandora's Box because these attackers can live in the secluded world of anonymity. With the advent of VOIP and the ability to spoof caller ID, as discussed in Chapter 5, anonymity is getting easier all the time; this advantage only increases with new and more interconnected technology. Then the combination of these two social engineering techniques in a set of attacks potentially represents a paradigm shift for security threat assessment.

Consider the growing problem of identity theft and the process a social engineer might adopt to facilitate the access to information. He or she might use the normal methods of direct observation of a site, facility, or group of employees. They might follow people when they go out for a drink after work and steal an ID badge or access pass from an employee during a momentary lapse of vigilance. Then they might call numerous people from the company's Web-based employee directory and ask them seemingly innocuous questions to gather structural data about reporting lines and the authority structure of the organization. They might do more electronic reconnaissance on the company Web site and the Internet. Combine this with compromising a network Web server to gather more sensitive information by capturing company e-mails and reading them. Finally, they complete their attack by strategically leveraging all this information to get a user ID and password to access a sensitive database or internal system. From this they gather customer or staff personal information sufficient to steal their identities and earn themselves hundreds of thousands of dollars. None of these events, individually, would likely provoke a momentous security reaction but, taken in concert, they represent a sizable security breach. This inequity between risk and loss events is the product of the multiplier of the cumulative converged risks.

Many of the well-known physical security scams and social engineering ploys have been around for a long time and are fairly well distributed among the general population. However, as we are starting to get a level of awareness in the physical realm, the cyber realm becomes a new delivery mechanism to reach millions of people quickly and cost-effectively. The commonplace "409 scam," often referred to as such because it originated from the 409 telephone area code, is a prime example of this transition. This fraud is typically perpetrated by a letter or information notice being received by the victim, promising that millions of dollars will be deposited in their bank account if the bank details are simply provided to the attacker. Although surely hundreds have probably fallen prey to this scam worldwide, it was more logistically challenging and costly to run this scam before the existence of the Internet. With the advent of e-mail, this scam can go on forever because there is no incremental cost to keep doing it! As long as e-mails can continually be sent to unsuspecting victims, the scam will likely continue. All the attacker needs is the computers to send the notices. The Bot nets discussed in the previous chapter are a great tool for distributing these e-mails. They are essentially anonymous because any trace will lead back to the unsuspecting owner of the compromised Bot computers. In the 1960s, social engineering had Frank Abagnale, recently portrayed in the 2002 movie *Catch Me If You Can*, as its poster child. In the 1990s, it was Kevin Mitnick and his brand of electronic social engineering. Both these former criminals exploited the same weakness: lack of security awareness by staff. The ability of security teams to work on converged threats and communicate comprehensive security messages will be an important task as technological advancements continue to enable integration and interconnectivity of systems and assets.

As mentioned earlier, another part of this unified voice is the communication to senior management. I do not know about your management teams, but mine do not have a lot of extra time and can often be challenged to give sufficient hours to hear separate messages from independent departments. By combining the reporting process to one session, even if delivered by two individuals, your management team's time spent on security can be optimized and, believe me, they will thank you for that. Maybe not in so many words, but they will be listening when you do come to speak because, if you do it right, it will be concise and focused at the enterprise level.

Conspicuously absent up to this point in the chapter has been any mention of technology cooperation, but this element creates a significant opportunity for the two groups to collaborate. Technologically and architecturally, these two security groups have many touch points where their systems often interact. These touch points are what I generally refer to as "convergence points" or points where the physical security systems and process interact with IT or IT security. Figure 12-1 is a diagram of some of these enterprise convergence points.

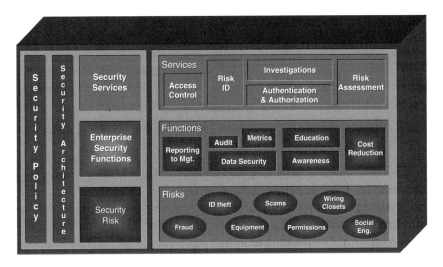

**Figure 12-1**   Enterprise convergence points.

As shown on the left side of the box, we can see security policy and security architecture that intersect with the entire enterprise security program. The top row of security services are common services that both departments perform and, in many cases, can be performed in concert with each other. Investigation is a common service that often contains both IT and physical elements. Enterprise security functions, as seen in the second row, are priorities, activities, or functions where the two groups can interact. We have already discussed education and awareness, but data security is one area where the end-to-end process requires a comprehensive effort. Even though data are secured electronically while on the servers, the servers themselves can be targeted and it must be physical security that prevents loss. Also, data backup tapes are frequently taken off-site from organizations and must be physically secured while in transit and in storage.

In the bottom row, we see the security risks and notice where the security risks the organization faces today have come together. These are excellent starting places for groups interested in cooperating on mitigating security risks. The risk item labeled Equipment refers to the loss of hardware and other equipment from the organization, either through malicious intent or accidental loss. Both groups can work to educate users on the protection of laptops, PDAs, cell phones, and other equipment, and regarding the risks to the organization should a device on which sensitive data stored be lost. Physical security groups can use their larger numbers of staff to identify equipment at risk while they are patrolling facilities, and then report this to the IT security team or engage the users themselves, if permitted, about the risk of loss. Although the convergence points diagram is neither exhaustive nor a panacea to beginning the convergence process, it is a tool to aid the user when thinking about convergence at the enterprise and security function levels.

# *Getting from Here to There*

# 13

## *How to Change*

The process of actually converging or integrating security teams or functions can be very different for organizations, depending on their size, structure, and political ability to adopt a new formation or process. Major obstacles to change can include turf wars, power struggles, fear, lack of defined goals, and lack of information, among many other challenges. The following chapters will hopefully support you in designing an approach that can aid you in avoiding some of these resistance points or at least navigate around the pointy ends of them. Although not all the ideas expressed in these plans are new or truly innovative, it is the dexterity with which one implements these ideas to address the challenge, not the mere existence of the characteristic. In other words, practice does not make security processes perfect; just repeated, correct practice moves your securityprogram towards perfection!

Once you are able to marshal all the necessary resources, skills, evidence, and support you need to make a strong case, agreement will likely follow. The remaining question is, What is needed in *your* environment? This requires detailed thought and analysis, reflection, and possibly outside assistance to get an honest assessment of your situation. Chapter 15 illustrates an organization-sized approach; although not all organizations will adopt a formal convergence project, many might choose instead to pick and choose some tasks or activities to achieve their own organizational benefit. Let us first start by looking at some best practice activities when preparing to make a change.

## ACQUIRE AN EXECUTIVE-LEVEL SPONSOR

Although hardly a new mantra in security management circles, this will likely be a key determinant in your success in trying to converge security functions. Executive-level support will be crucial at many times during the convergence process, but will be most prominent when winning the initial support and defining your project charter. The sponsor can also be helpful when dealing with departmental or business unit resistance, and in persuading concurrence during large steps or evolutions within the project's progression.

Getting a project charter is a fundamental step in your project success. A convergence project is not a simple matter, devoid of complexity and political minefields. Your project charter must be achievable given the time, resources, and expectations present in your organization. You must be able to identify your responsibility and authority, the scope and objectives of the project, and any formal independence you have in order to make organizational changes. Although convergence benefits can be powerful and compelling, you might indeed need the ability to compel business groups to participate and work with you. For instance, if you need to gather metrics in building your business case on the existing cost of access control breach incidents in your organization, you might need to compel the IT group to provide the data, without which you might have difficulty in making a sanguine argument for integrated identity management. As convergence projects generally cross departmental lines, your charter should clearly state the reporting lines for the project leader and identify the stakeholders. Finally, your convergence project charter should clearly define what project completion will look like. These types of change projects are highly susceptible to "scope creep,"[1] and having a clear set of milestones and success factors will let you declare success at some point in the future.

---

[1]Scope Creep: Unplanned expansion in a project's scope.

The executive-level sponsor will need to be fully apprised of the project progress so they can support you during senior leadership discussions, strategy sessions, and budget debates. Although milestone completion and project successes must be rigorously reported to senior management, your project sponsor should be the first to know when a benefit has been gained. They will be able to aid you in presenting the information in the most effective manner for your organization. Much of the selling of any new program is about packaging and positioning: if a message is packaged well and positioned with all necessary sensitivities, the message will be received well. If you go through the trouble of ensuring that you have thought through others' concerns in advance, there is a high probability that you will not find yourself surprised in the process with something you had not considered. For example, when I was thinking about how to begin selling the concept of utilizing my corporate guard force for IT security compliance work, I was led to consider how significant are the roles these people play in our organization and how these people were being underutilized. This, in turn, led me to the position of using the existing guard resources, adding some training to their skill sets, and getting true risk mitigation for no incremental cost; this is an easy argument to support with obvious benefits. Once you have your executive sponsor, a clear, concise, and cogent vision must be developed.

## DRAFT THE NEW VISION

The importance of having a clear and well-articulated vision for change cannot be overstated. Convergence is often a bit of a mystery, so defining exactly what your new vision is can be difficult yet extremely crucial. You hear a lot about vision statements in business, and there are as many definitions as there are visions. I have heard vision referred to as "the desired future state of the organization." I have also read that when Fortune 500 CEOs were polled about why their vision was not achieved, most of them identified "a failure to implement the vision" as the reason for failure. My view is that in drafting a vision for your project, you should focus on the desired outcomes you want to achieve, while keeping a clear understanding of what is achievable given your organization and situation. My vision for our organization was to create one enterprise-wide security function wherein processes and technology are integrated, people are trained and utilized fully, while minimizing the senior management time required yet increasing their awareness; an organization wherein all security risks are identified through comprehensive, repeatable, and verifiable assessment and investigation techniques. Finally, I wanted to ensure that security costs to the organization were minimized where possible.

## HAVE A SOLID CHANGE MANAGEMENT PLAN

Any time there are changing or shifting roles in an organization, there will be some confusion and a little fear. During the transition and education period, it is imperative to have a solid change management plan. Addressing issues such as the potential impact to people's roles, lives, and jobs, up-front in the project plan, will help in easing the transition. Some organizations have combined the security control room with the IT security monitoring function. The difference between monitoring door alarms, panic and fire alarms, and attempts to launch a denial of service (DoS) attack against the firewall is considerable. Retraining staff is no small effort and will likely play on some deep fears of the people involved. If they are physical security staff, they might have no idea what a DoS is and even less of an idea what to do about it. They are accustomed to seeing a door alarm and dispatching a guard or the police, making a report, and moving on to the next incident. The process of actively monitoring a firewall and activating an IT incident response program will give the most seasoned physical security professional a sense of pause. By the same token, an IT person might not have a full appreciation for the importance of what the panic alarm entails and might have to be educated on the truly important sense of personal safety that the alarm is indicating—where someone's life may hang in the balance. For me, it was essential to ensure that all staff knew up-front, and repeating on numerous occasions, that the convergence project was not about downsizing or job loss. Rather, this would be a good thing for them. Not only would they be learning new skills and be gaining a greater appreciation for the overall security of the entire organization, they would also be helping to reduce the risk all staff and visitors face when interacting with our organization.

An essential component of the change management plan is to ensure that you have the liaison relationships set up with the necessary functional departments so you can easily acquire answers to questions that might come during the project. In union organizations, alterations to work routines and duties may spur the union local to ask for a job reclassification or review to see whether the new role rates a compensation or band review; letting human resources know about this in advance will accelerate the response to these questions. As the overall security mandate begins to change over time, you may have budget implications, so having open discussions with finance could become very helpful. Only you will know which relationships are fundamental to your success, but by determining them in advance you will be further ahead.

## ATTAIN SENIOR MANAGEMENT BUY-IN

Although you have already acquired your executive sponsor, developed your new vision, and prepared your change management strategy, it is vital to attain senior management buy-in as soon as possible. My belief is that if you can show them how much less of their time you will need under this program, you will be off to a great start. Consider the amount of time two separate security departments require from senior management for activities such as:

- Reporting new security risks
- Status reports
- Metrics reporting
- Business cases
- Security awareness
- Education sessions
- Risk assessments
- Investigations results
- Risk management discussions
- Budget discussions
- Security implications of new projects or acquisitions
- Many more

Just the time each department spends informing and interacting with senior management is a staggering number of hours, and if you could reduce that by 30–50% this will likely be a huge motivator for them; this frees them up to do the rest of their work.

Senior management buy-in, however you attain it, is essential because some folks will support or rebuff you as you trek through the project. They will need to see benefits—see them soon, and often. Not only are you going to look like a forward-thinking star for championing this cause, you can rightly claim the results of your efforts to reduce bureaucracy and duplication, which translates into saving money and reducing risk. If you have a decentralized security operation with many business units, each with senior leaders with whom you cannot regularly get face time, metrics are going to be critical for you. Some objective measure that shows risk being reduced and costs being managed in an innovative manner will aid you in setting the stage with these decentralized leaders.

One tool that may be helpful in communicating security risk to these folks is a "security dashboard," which could be available with the combined security measures of the organization in real time. Some kind of an aggregate scoring, similar to the Department of Homeland Security's yellow/orange/red color scheme, may be helpful in quickly communicating the risk level at that moment to the executive. This would give the executive the ability to see enterprise security incidents that have occurred in their sphere of influence and give them the ability to interact with and get more information on these issues. Some organizations will give executives the ability to click from the dashboard and see security incident reports; from there they can activate a CCTV camera and zoom right in on the area where the incident occurred to judge for themselves whether it is an issue for their concern. Likewise, if they see on their dashboard that virus attacks blocked at the firewall are up 30% in the past quarter, they might be more inclined to hear your proposal to increase funding for antivirus defenses. Whatever the techniques you choose to get senior management involved and win their buy-in, you must remember that this buy-in must be sustained with results, so ensure that their expectations are managed accordingly.

## STRATEGIC REVIEW OR INVENTORY OF ASSETS

The next step in preparing for convergence is to conduct a truly honest review or inventory of the assets you have available.

Exploring and understanding the technology, budget, people, and skill sets available to you is crucial because the convergence process is essentially about finding how to best utilize your assets in an ultra-efficient manner to reduce the security risk across the organization. This is often where some creativity enters your convergence project.

It is my advice that you start with your most vital asset, your people. One of the first things I realized shortly into my journey toward convergence was that one of my key resources was not going to get onboard the convergence train. He was too "old school" and had done things his way for too long. To this day, I am still not sure whether he was just not interested in changing or was afraid of the technology aspects of the project, but one thing was clear: he didn't like my ideas on enterprise-wide security. Although I tried to get him to willingly participate in the conversions, this was received with a great deal of passive-aggressive resistance. I learned something valuable during that time: sometimes during central or strategic change, you just might have to change some of the people. Although it was neither pleasant nor inexpensive, he had to go! If you have decided that convergence is the right thing for your organization, you might face some of the same responses and might have to make a tough decision or two.

Given that you have your team onboard with your vision, you might then have to start the process of helping them develop new skills. This may be enhancing new skills, building team skills, hiring outside people with the critical skills you need, or even bringing in consulting skills at various stages of the process. Please see the case study discussion later in this chapter for some examples of these types of skills we needed early on in our own convergence project. It is essential to recognize the level, mix, and balance of skills you have at your disposal. I was pleasantly surprised to learn that one of my supervisors in the security guard department had a background and credentials in computer crime investigation from the military—certainly not something I initially expected.

In completing the process of evaluating the skill sets available, I have found that a matrix approach can be helpful. Please see Table 13-1. As you see in the matrix, I suggest starting with a realistic assessment of your team's skills. Start with a list down the left side, the skills you need specific to your organization. You may

**Table 13-1** Skills Matrix

| | Employee #1 | Employee #2 | Employee #3 | Employee #4 |
|---|---|---|---|---|
| Access control Systems | 1 | 1 | | |
| Application Security | | | 1 | |
| Business Continuity Planning | | 1 | 3 | |
| Computer Forensics | | | 1 | |
| Risk Assessment | | 2 | | |
| Legal Issues | 2 | 2 | | |
| Emergency Management Practices | | | | 1 |
| Records Mgt. | | | | 1 |
| Industrial Security | | | | 1 |
| Information Security | 2 | | 1 | |
| Investigations | | 2 | 2 | |
| CCTV | | | | 2 |
| Personnel Security | 3 | | 2 | |
| Physical Security Planning | | 3 | | 2 |
| Regulatory & Compliance Mgt. | | | 3 | |
| Security Architecture | 3 | | 3 | |

choose to separate these items into traditional subjects of IT and physical security or another structure. Next, list your staff names across the top of the matrix; and finally, fill out the matrix. Place a 1 in each box for advanced skills in a discipline, a 2 in each box where the person has moderate knowledge in a subject area, and a 3 in each box where the person has fundamental skill levels.

Now that you have your people's levels of skills, you can use this information to analyze the mix of people and skills you have available to you. You might find there is concentration in one area or another, such as investigations or risk assessment. Although this may be fine for the traditional environment, if you are planning to move to a one-card solution for access control you might need staff to have a better understanding of technology to facilitate the new access control processes. Likewise, if you plan to integrate your investigations function but your IT security staff has limited experience in this area (all having rated a 1 on the matrix), you might need to address this skill development via training or education.

This matrix, or your analysis, might be useful in determining the training required for your staff. It might help you identify who should be cross-trained or who needs further education. This might allow you to focus your decision making on training and education budget priorities over the next few years of your convergence journey. When completing your analysis, one exercise that might become useful is a realistic review of how to best use your people. Convergence projects may be easy or difficult to define, but project leaders can be selected from either group, and this process may help you decide who is best placed based on their skill sets. Now certainly other factors can play into these decisions, such as rank, project management skills, desire, and individual competency, but I have found that in this process I learned things about my new aggregate staff I did not know when they were separated by department, and this led to my making decisions differently regarding whom I chose to lead which projects.

In reviewing the technology you have to work with, it is necessary to understand that it is not always financially feasible to tear out corporate systems and start from scratch. Mechanisms such as internal planning processes, governance structures, and formal or informal interaction rituals may be key factors to take into account when considering modifications to technology for convergence. Internal planning mechanisms, such as capital budget cycles, can be key factors in understanding when the technology component of your convergence plan may be implemented. Other processes, such as management meetings and strategic planning cycles, may also be significant mechanisms to understand when considering technology modifications or enhancements. Further, there might be human resource implications when considering integrating some systems, such as one-card access control systems; these often have duplicate staff to maintain independent systems which sometimes, as a product of integration, can be affected. It might be crucial to consider carefully the existing IT governance structure when formulating technology integration plans. In our organization there is a separate technology governance structure and, when considering technology integration, these groups might need to be consulted early in the process. My experience has shown that IT people often have other considerations to offer to your program which you might not have thought of, such as technology life cycle management, obsolescence and refresh scheduling, and network management considerations. In my experience there are often common architectures that security technology systems conform to inside an organization.

## COMPLETELY SEPARATE NETWORKS

In some organizations, where security infrastructures grew organically, you might have a situation where none of the existing physical security systems run on the corporate data network. Although it is common today to see some level of integration, I know of organizations still using this type of architecture. This type of configuration can offer some level of protection not available to integrated systems. Commonly referred to as "security through obscurity," this type of setup is not subject to all the same vulnerabilities as integrated systems since they generally do not run on the same wires as other network computers. The proliferation of personal computer (PC) technology has created a situation where massive groups of computers on a network can be attacked simultaneously and every computer on that network can be vulnerable. With completely separate networks, this risk is considerably diminished. Although this can offer some comfort to security managers in this situation, in reality the peril can only be avoided for a short time. As more and more security systems begin to rely on standard operating systems such as Microsoft Windows, and these systems are connected to the Internet for ease of maintenance, the weaknesses experienced by the data network begin to creep into the environment. So although the separate network might not be as subject to traditional IT security attacks such as viruses, Trojan horses, and worms, it is only a matter of time until obsolescence, cost, or the need to be integrated with other networks or organizations push these IT practitioners to accept network integration.

One of the more common configurations found in growing corporate security organizations is the partially integrated network, where only some of the physical security systems are operating across the data network and sharing network resources. Some legacy systems[‡] might still operate separately from the data network due to the cost of integrating or other reasons; intrusion alarms that use telephone dialers to call for assistance are common examples. This might include the use of standard operating systems and the data network as the transport system to connect access control panels and CCTV to their applications. This is generally easy to accomplish because all it requires is a connection to the network and some basic configuration.

This is the beginning of the organizational benefits gained by leveraging the data network. By not having a duplicate copper or fiber connection, the organization reduces these associated installation and maintenance costs and begins to harness more of the value from the modern physical security system. Typically, in these configurations we still find nonstandard (i.e., non-organization) equipment such as servers and desktops being used. This is often the case because the security vendor packages its products already installed on hardware. This can add numerous challenges, not the least of which comes when modifications need to be made to the application or operating system. If an update needs to be applied to these third party-supplied systems, often the vendor must be called to complete this work. This solution does not scale well because applying this approach to large quantities of systems can be time-consuming and financially intensive. Another characteristic common to this class of network is that when these systems are installed they are often exposed to direct attack or risk because they are not segmented[2] from the rest of the network. Major challenges can occur in this type of configuration, because physical security system service outages often are a combination of problems, and finding one group to admit they are responsible for fixing the problem in a timely fashion can be problematic.

For most organizations, the ideal method to fully leverage the investment in technology is to move to a fully integrated

---

[‡]Legacy systems: Typically an older computer or information system maintained by the business organization for a specific business reason, such as replacement is not desirable because of cost or effort, or a replacement system is not yet available.
[2]Segmentation: Physically and logically separating one segment of the network from another. Often done by inserting a firewall between the two network segments.

network. In this environment we find standard servers and PCs being used for all security systems. Vendor applications run on organization-approached hardware, and are generally managed and maintained centrally. Service level agreements between departments, which clearly specify roles, responsibilities, and processes for escalation system problems, are common features of this type of configuration. One of the greatest benefits of the fully integrated approach within the organization is that a platform is created upon which to begin converging IT and physical security systems, such as access control, intrusion detection, and metrics management. Many of the typical corporate tools operated by IT departments can be incredibly helpful to corporate security groups, such as antivirus and antispyware systems, patch management, and data backup and recovery.

One of the main challenges with this approach is that it can have security issues. The fully integrated network often ends up with IT personnel managing the technology environment in which the physical security systems operate. Getting IT personnel background checks done can often be troublesome, especially in an environment where these positions are part of the collective bargaining unit. But even if these people are not union members, they might not consent to having their job changed to one that requires police record checks, credit history reviews, and other standard background checks to be completed. The difficulty is that these individuals usually have administrator access to your security systems equipment. Now you are faced with a risk decision related to your level of trust in people either new to your team or with whom you might have had very little contact. To confuse matters further, these administrators may have privileges such that they can bypass or erase audit measures such as logging or auditing systems. In evaluating how you will approach convergence, you can gain significant benefit from reviewing the processes of security and how they are affected by convergence.

# The Process Approach   **14**

The IT environment, in the majority of cases, is a process-oriented place. There are processes for application development, system deployment, quality assurance, and maintenance. The same can be said of physical security in large, complex environments. Organizations such as the military or McDonald's both embrace process because they can attain the benefits that process delivers quite easily by simply engendering repeatability, verifiability, and reliability in the manner in which activities are performed. In security, we like repeatable, verifiable, and reliable things because they usually deliver results we can count on, and when you count on a function for life safety or risk reduction, its importance is amplified.

Security practitioners will often be heard evangelizing that security is a process and not a state of being or an end point. Although this is true, it is not enough to refer to security as a process, since all of the activities in the security program need to become processes that have defined beginnings and end points. The benefits of creating and continuously improving the process can include improved quality, reduced cost, and decreased cycle time of the activity. This is especially significant when looking at convergence from the perspective of it not occurring overnight.

There are a number of process-driven activities in security functions, including security strategy development, policy development, investigations, and risk assessment. Each of these processes provides an opportunity to begin down the convergence avenue. This is what I like to think of as my "creeping incrementalism" approach to convergence. Start with one activity that makes sense to converge, or even when a security policy could benefit from integration, and work together to develop something that delivers value to the organization. In the case of a policy under development, this may be that the policy development team reduced the amount of time it took to complete the policy, or, if this was an IT security policy, the avoidance of having to create a duplicate policy for physical security.

For example, assume that new legislation or an audit requirement states that you must develop an organizational security policy for the control of personally identifiable information within your company. This kind of information often comes in physical as well as electronic form, so both the physical and IT security departments might have concerns. Physical security might want a policy that defines a clean desk policy and other rules pertaining to securing filing cabinets. The IT security staff will likewise be interested in where this information is stored and how it is transmitted. To meet the audit or legislation requirement in a diverged environment, you might get two groups developing corporate policies in near isolation. In the converged world, you can simply reorient the policy development process to factor in all issues related to the security of personally identifiable information. You might begin by classifying personal information (in whatever form) as sensitive or protected data. Then your team could identify all the sources for this information and how they are used. Next, the team could go through the issues, both physical and IT, where the information could be at risk. The last step will be to draft a policy and present it to management and the stakeholders for discussion and approval. The result is a comprehensive security policy that meets all the needs of the business requirement, considers all risks for the assets, and reduces the amount of stakeholder time (by up to 50%) necessary to evaluate the policy viability and appropriateness. This delivers true-value risk mitigation and has decreased the cost and cycle time necessary to complete the activity.

Once this is complete, the first converged process has been created for the organization, with a defined beginning and end. You can now begin to build the necessary characteristics into the process to make it easily repeatable, verifiable, and eventually reliable. When this is reviewed over the term of many years and activities, real value can be measured.

Reduced management and stakeholder time and reduced cycle time of process development can become incredibly beneficial when you take on activities such as strategic plan development. These plans are usually developed annually, so they are ideal for process improvement activities. They involve the collection of input data, analysis, recommendations, and the creation of a tactical plan for implementation. Given that both departments probably do something (even informally) that resembles this activity, convergence can offer great benefits in this endeavour.

When developing strategic plans, one of the more common discussions is around cost control or reduction. Given that I have yet to meet a security group leader with an unlimited budget, I will assume for the sake of this discussion that we are all in the same budgetary boat. When you bring your IT and physical security professionals together in the strategic discussion and start brainstorming, you can begin by discussing the major cost centers in your budgets and the major business and cost drivers relevant to you. Think about this from the perspective of physical security storage requirements and the cost to purchase CCTV storage for video images. You can purchase multiple digital video recorders (DVRs) at more than $10,000 each to store CCTV data, pay a vendor to maintain and service them, and spend thousands of more dollars to build redundant capacity into the system for emergency management and business continuity purposes. The alternative in a convergence discussion might be to only purchase DVRs for locations which have a justifiable business need to have local access at all times, and then archive the balance of your CCTV data on the IT storage area network (SAN). For the uninitiated, the SAN is a large array of inexpensive storage disks that can store your video for probably a third of the cost of DVR storage, while probably giving you all your maintenance and redundancy for free or a low maintenance fee.

The benefit here is that the SAN is already in place in the IT department, storing millions of bytes of data, and it does not care what kind of data you have. You just purchase a separate set of storage disks for your images and configure the route for images to be stored there. Now, in practice the process is more complex than it sounds, but the point is that a combined approach to resolving previously independent budget challenges can have new life breathed into them by joint discussions and planning.

Another interesting benefit of convergence, aside from saving money, reducing time and effort, and optimizing cycle time, is that you can also achieve higher risk mitigation through increased frequency of new, comprehensive activities, such as risk assessments and security reviews. Risk assessments can be a large and formal process or an automated tool run by a consultant on one piece of your organization, but generally they are focused on assessing pieces of the pie when it comes to the risks your organizations faces. In our organization, as it may be in yours, risk assessments tend to be less frequent in the IT environment as compared to the physical environment. IT tends to have "limited feet on the ground," meaning fewer people to go out and conduct risk assessments. When thinking about all the aspects of IT security we would like to assess on a more frequent basis, we discovered that many IT security items could be identified that we could build into the physical risk assessment process when evaluating a building or other physical space, such as network wall jacks, laptops, universal serial bus (USB) tokens, server rooms, wiring closets, and many other risks. This is especially viable when your organization is a large, decentralized group where IT security staff does not often visit the physical buildings. By enhancing the risk assessment process with additional questions, criteria, training, and tools, you can increase the frequency of risk assessments and probably increase risk mitigation for a negligible incremental cost.

After each one of these small wins, you can evangelize the value of convergence in your organization, declare success, and continue on in your creeping incrementalism process approach to convergence. There are many other security processes you can review in your organization; you simply need to start the conversation between security groups, recognize the benefits as having value to you and your organization, and use your creativity to get started.

# 15

# *The Organization Size Approach*

I believe that the size of the organization is not necessarily a key determining factor of whether convergence can be achieved. In my experience, integrating services or departments is more about collaboration and strategic thinking. When you combine these two characteristics with an organization's will to change, and add people without their egos at play, the opportunity exists to make decisions that will enable the business to embrace enterprise risk mitigation. I reiterate: It is not about size; it's about working together, using complementary skills and strategic thinking, and working through the challenges that are unique to each size of organization.

Smaller organizations have fewer dedicated security staff and overall fewer resources with which to work. They might have difficulty accessing the capital needed to fund extensive convergence projects, or the expertise needed to explore the complexity of integrating complex IT systems. On the other hand, because they are smaller they may be more nimble and can more easily change direction, and they have fewer stakeholders to convince that convergence is a worthwhile endeavor. Although the fewer resources might limit the size of projects they can take on, this does not limit some of the quick wins they can attain from exploring the enterprise security risks they face.

Medium-sized organizations will usually have some resources that the smaller organizations do not. For example, they may have a dedicated security manager for both IT and physical security, their own corporate security force, as well as a robust or maturing corporate security program. Such an organization will generally have both financial- and expertise-related resources, and will likely be open to a sophisticated or best practice approach to deploying resources and mitigating risk. These medium-sized organizations that want to sustain growth and protect brand equity must avoid a public security breach. These organizations are probably the best candidates for a complete convergence of IT and physical security since they are likely not too large and decentralized to hinder the convergence process. They tend to still be flexible enough that making significant enterprise changes can be accomplished within a matter of months, not years.

Large-sized organizations have significant resources they can bring to bear on these projects. They usually will have dedicated security resources throughout the organization and other ancillary resources that are helpful, such as project management, business analysts, and "line of business" consultants. These team members will become especially useful in the data gathering and analysis phases of any major convergence projects. They are necessary in large organizations because, although the degree of change in one project might not be vast, the lateral scope of the project might be significant across many business units or lines of business, subsidiaries, outsource partners, and geographical jurisdiction and legal structures. So, although these larger organizations offer the most resources to be dedicated to these projects, they also likely have the most complexity, which might make convergence seem like an enormous and even daunting task. Further, they might have very rigid silos between physical and IT security groups where the cultures are more ingrained and organizational politics are most entrenched and least magnanimous.

The key to remember is that convergence needs to be slow and measured; you need to start with the quick wins wherever you can and look for the low-hanging fruit—the easy pickings. So what specifically, then, can each of these large-sized organizations do to achieve any degree of convergence?

## SMALL COMPANIES

For the sake of this discussion, let us define small companies as firms with revenues up to $100 million. They often can easily start down the path of convergence due to their inherent nimbleness and ability to react well to changing conditions. Although they might not be able to or it might not make sense to attempt all the convergence activities discussed in this chapter, they can certainly focus themselves on the low–cost projects. Given that they might not have any dedicated security resources other than contract security staff, or possibly a corporate security officer, they can first try to ensure that they are fully leveraging their IT infrastructure to manage the physical security systems they have in place. Duplicate infrastructures used to operate the access control, CCTV, and alarm reporting system are low-hanging fruit. Line managers can work with IT staff to see that the physical security computer systems are appropriately managed. This might mean using the IT patch management system to ensure that security computers are appropriately patched and protected from viruses, Trojan horses, and worms. These computers need to be reviewed to make certain that nonessential IT services are shut down to minimize internal users from being able to exploit vulnerabilities in the equipment.

Given the compact size of the small company, it will be much simpler than in large organizations to enunciate the messages of security awareness. It will be even easier if the frequency of messages is optimized by ensuring the quality, comprehensiveness, and integrated nature of the messages. If the facilities or human resources departments are responsible for physical security, they could work with the IT group (which may or may not be responsible for IT security) to simply combine the two messages into one communication. People tend to tune out messages if they are too frequent and overbearing. By optimizing the number of messages, it is much more likely that they are focused on the key security messages, whatever they are, thus making great advances in the security awareness program.

Although you might not have the benefit of your own corporate security staff in this size of organization, you can work with your contract guard provider to expand the role they play in observing and reporting security risks. One of the main functions of the roving security guard is to observe and report conditions in the environment they are protecting. They historically focus on traditional security matters, such as unsafe conditions, suspicious activities, and persons attending the physical site. With minimal training, these personnel can be trained to observe and report rudimentary IT security risks. Now I can hear some of you already saying "No way, these people are not going near IT." But I assure you that this is a completely safe and sensible tactic, if done right.

There are three main conditions I would have contract guards immediately trained to report in this small business environment. The first condition relates to insecure IT systems or equipment. I have frequently seen wiring closets (which often provide access to network drops and phone systems) left open by contractors. This condition is risky and can easily be logged by a security guard for review by the facilities or IT department the next day. Computer servers are key pieces of network infrastructure and habitually contain sensitive information, yet on occasion are left in compromising positions. In one organization in which I was employed, I found a remote "active directory" server balancing on a garbage can (still plugged in and running) because the closet in which it was located was under construction at the time. For physical security practitioners, this would be akin to taking your access control computer, logging in, and leaving it out for anyone to access. These kinds of vulnerabilities, though hopefully rare, represent conditions that security staff can report. We are only talking about observing and reporting these conditions, not touching anything! Once these conditions have been reported, they can be resolved or dealt with by the appropriate staff member.

Another idea for the smaller organization is the concept of a Risk Council. Given that you might not have specific subject matter expertise dedicated to security on staff, another approach for organizations that are serious about protecting their assets and information would be to form a multi-stakeholder internal group to discuss security risks the organization faces. This might include requirements the firm must meet under prevailing legislation, protections required to protect sensitive or personally identifiable data such as credit card information, or the number of suspicious persons witnessed hanging around the buildings after hours. For further discussion on small business options for convergence, please see Chapter 18.

## MEDIUM-SIZED ORGANIZATIONS

Let us define medium-sized companies as those businesses with annual revenue of $100 million to $1 billion, or a local or state government. Certainly, such entities offer more resources than do smaller companies, including dedicated security staff with subject matter expertise, more extensive budgets, access to capital funding, and probably enhanced security business drivers such as privacy or financial legislation commitments. Having access to expertise creates the opportunity to focus on the strategic planning component of convergence. Dedicated resources can allocate time to exploring, in detail, opportunities for risk mitigation through convergence. This might be through organizing a small project team or a work group to review security threats and risks, and working through the approach planned for each department. This strategic plan will also provide a launching platform from which to initiate the discussion on convergence with senior management.

Many mid-sized organizations will have access to in-house physical security forces, which can be the starting point for picking the low-hanging fruit of risk mitigation. As described in the small business section, utilizing the guard force to observe and report IT security infractions or policy breaches is a simple and low-cost convergence activity. With your in-house guard force you can then expand this role to look for more worrisome breaches, such as rogue wireless access points or passwords left on written notes around work surfaces. In many environments the IT security group will have policies restricting the use of wireless routers on the data network. These routers are reasonably small and can be hidden in an office rather easily. Staff will often plug one of these routers into the network (in violation of policy) because they are easy to buy and deploy in their own space. This leaves the IT environment with a back door into the data network with little or no protection—potentially creating a significant risk for IT. Equipping the guard force with the description of these devices and a $40 hand-held wireless "sniffer" can enable them to locate these devices. Again, I reiterate to abate your fears: They do not have to touch anything—simply observe and report. The IT group can investigate on the next business day.

As for passwords that have been written down, this is probably one of the most common problems that is collectively shared by most organizations. It presents a significant risk to everyone. Given the growing interconnectivity of business systems, this often can lead to unintentional risks being absorbed by the business with little additional recognition of that risk. The security guard can simply observe the desktop spaces and check the usual suspect locations, such as under every user's keyboard or mouse pad to see whether any user information is present.

This mid-sized organization usually will have a robust IT infrastructure with expansive data storage and backup and recovery capability. This provides a significant opportunity for the physical security staff to leverage this storage space to increase reliability and availability of security records and to lower costs. One of the main IT network storage devices used is called a SAN. For physical security practitioners, this is, in effect, a huge storage device where records can be stored and accessed as required, but at a much lower price point than traditional file server storage. Instead of proliferating DVRs across the organization (which require regular maintenance and replacement), CCTV files can be stored on the SAN. The files will remain backed-up, maintained, available, and safe and the cost of storage will probably be less than half that of the traditional DVR storage. Now this might not work in all situations, such as where on-site storage is needed, but it can aid in drastically reducing your operating costs for CCTV. Although physical security hardware vendors will not like this too much, it can be useful in many situations, and only a little research and discussion will be able to tell you whether this is right for your organization. One important note here is that this does not absolve you of the responsibility to ensure that access controls and protections are in place in this IT environment; it is simply a more efficient method of storage. You must consider who should have access to this data, what the backgrounds of the system administrators are, whether there are any privacy impacts of this new solution, and any other issues relevant to your environment.

Another cooperation opportunity at this level of organization is the assessment of security risk. Risk assessments are generally performed on a regular or semi-regular basis in organizations of this size. A number of options present themselves when dissecting the security risk assessment process in mid-sized firms, and the first option is how and when they will be utilized. Physical security risk assessments often are regular activities that are performed on physical facilities annually or biannually, and involve the traditional review of physical risks to the environment and the assets. The IT security risk assessments usually happen less frequently at this level, if at all, and often are a response to an incident or an audit requirement. The reason for this is often that they are complex to complete, time-consuming, and generally require a fair amount of technical expertise and knowledge of the environment. This does create a problem in that the physical security protections of the technology often go unassessed for extended periods of time.

One approach we have adopted in our organization is the integration of these physical aspects of the IT systems into the physical security risk assessment process. When a physical risk assessment is completed in a building, the consultant also reviews conditions for risks to the physical security of the IT systems. Earlier I used the example of a server balancing on a garbage can; this is a prime example of a converged risk that can be assessed. Other risks to be reviewed include the number of laptops present that are not locked up or secured, versus recent thefts in your organization and the surrounding area. With a little added expertise, the assessor could take a laptop computer and plug into wall ports in public and unoccupied private areas such as board rooms to determine whether they can get an Internet connection or can "see" the network.

Another opportunity that might present itself is unification of the reporting structure so that security groups can report to one CSO. Now I know that this is a sore point for many people and many disagree with this idea entirely, but it is possible to do, so hear me out before you start flipping pages. More and more these days, we see one leader for both security functions, and this does make sense in the right situations. Either you must have one individual, like myself, who understands and speaks both physical security and "techie," or you need a CSO who has talented subject matter experts reporting to him or her; either way, this can work. There are many advantages to the converged reporting structure, including the ability to maintain a harmonized strategic planning process and a single and transparent reporting line to senior management that allows for a comprehensive and fused enterprise security message to be reported.

Conflict can occur when independent security structures report security risks in different ways, and senior management is left to try and determine the highest priority. Which issue represents the highest risk to the organization? Imagine two risks being presented to senior management simultaneously: One needs to address cyber attacks that could take down the network and interrupt business, and the other is a potential brewing workplace violence issue. How can senior management prioritize these issues correctly when they are not risk experts? Further, how do they balance the prevailing budget and compensating control opportunities? The independent reporting structure, although effective in many ways, does not address all the management issues involved in leading an enterprise security function. Nevertheless, it does leave room for the unified reporting structure to deliver business value; it just has to be done correctly by people with the applicable expertise and education for these new and growing integrated threats. For security practitioners, this presents a significant opportunity to begin learning about the security issues that affect the entire enterprise, by attaining new security credentials and attending professional security development opportunities in areas of security that they are less familiar with. In case you missed it, this topic is explored further in Chapter 10.

## LARGE ORGANIZATIONS

Let us define large organizations as businesses with annual revenues in excess of $1 billion dollars, or a federal government. These are the most blessed with resources but often are the most challenged to formally converge their security structures. These organizations have probably had independent security structures for many years and likely are even operating in different business units. They may have numerous subsidiaries or outsource partners and may extend across multiple continents and legal jurisdictions. The benefits of being able to bring formal project teams together with dedicated project management resources is undeniably ideal when it comes to planning a convergence process, but the structure of a global organization can be crushing when it comes to gaining stakeholder buy-in and concurrence. If the organization has followed the proper steps, as discussed in Chapter 13, it is probably well on its way to being successful at its project. But to attempt convergence in an ad hoc manner at this level is, in my opinion, twaddle. Organizational change of any kind needs support, and when you are talking about changing people's job roles or functions, it is critical.

In my research for this book, I observed a large organization that had converged its security control center and its network security function. One set of staff was standing guard to respond to network intrusions as well as physical intrusions. This is an amazing accomplishment, which no doubt was achieved through a tremendous amount of support, training, and willpower. Although this might not work for every organization, it is possible to do if you can get past the overarching education, process, technical, and human resource issues. Before you toss this book aside and brand it rubbish for even suggesting the idea, remember that it is this kind of creativity that is saving organizations tens of thousands of dollars and reducing risk every day.

Another opportunity for integration is in the collection, analysis, and reporting of security metrics. Although both IT and physical security practitioners seem to collect and report security metrics to senior management, there is a genuine opportunity to optimize management time by integrating metrics reporting. The other benefit is that the integrated metrics report provides a more comprehensive view of the organization's true security risk position. This might aid you in selling the security message to senior management when you present the information in a comprehensive form, thereby reducing their time required to engage in the process. This topic leads back to the previous discussion of the reporting structure, and I will not open that wound again lest I be branded a zealot, but this is another example of where the single report can optimize the security message.

## INVESTIGATIONS

The final convergence topic I will explore in this chapter is investigation. Investigations are generally conducted by both security groups which, more often than not these days, cross paths as many threats and improper activities involve actions in both the physical and IT worlds.

- Harassment and stalking cases at work generally start in the physical realm and at some point migrate to e-mail.
- People running extraneous businesses from their company desktop inevitably end up crossing into both worlds.
- Most internal fraud activities have an electronic trail that needs to be followed.

These examples illustrate that separate investigation processes just do not make good sense any more. It is no longer good enough for investigators to paw through PCs looking for evidence—and in the process destroy any forensic evidence in the files. By bringing the two investigation groups together, they can learn a great deal from each other and increase the assurance level that a proper investigation has been conducted. Physical investigators can teach IT security staff more about continuity of evidence and preparing for court, whereas IT security investigators can teach their counterparts about forensic issues and the proper way to engage IT tools to capture and record crucial electronic evidence.

Although large organizations can be challenging environments when initiating change, they offer the greatest opportunities for cost optimization and infrastructure leveraging.

# 16

# *The Methodological Approach*

Now that you have your convergence project defined, or at least have an agreement for two or more departments to work together, we can look at a base methodology to approach convergence. This is not a "one size fits all" solution; there are a few steps to consider following. In the end, your project plan might be driven by a formal project management methodology with defined milestones and deliverables but, if not, this may be helpful.

## STEP 1. PROJECT KICK-OFF MEETING

Start by bringing your group of interested parties together to begin discussing how you will approach convergence. It will be helpful to first define the four Ws (who, what, where, and when) of the project. This is an important step because "scope creep" can easily enter projects that deliver positive benefits to an organization. As you begin a convergence project, it is likely that you are going to discover many other opportunities for efficiency and savings. My advice is to not try and do everything at once. Simply record the findings and move on to completing your defined project. It will be critical in most organizations to complete the project, record the successes, and evangelize the results across the organization. Please remember my comments from earlier in the book that convergence must be slow and measured. Too much change can be deadly to any project and, although the benefits of convergence will likely speak for themselves, if you can sustain benefits and report continual successes over extended periods of time, you are likely to continue to receive senior management support when you later recommend more complex projects that might be more contentious.

The first W will be Who, so initially you need to decide who will be participating in the project. Identifying who the project leader will be is crucial and, in the beginning of your new relationship, both departments might want to share the leadership of the endeavor. This is fine as long as there are goals, tasks, and deliverables all clearly laid out. Projects that are more technical in nature might lend themselves to IT-savvy individuals leading them because they will probably have experience with the kinds of issues that can challenge these assignments. Projects that are more people- or process-oriented may be good opportunities for physical security leaders to direct, as they tend to lend themselves to cross-department, people-oriented activities that are commonly found in the physical security realm.

Another Who topic might be who will be assisting as a subject matter expert or consultant on the project. If there is someone from another organization or a local consultant who has experience in convergence projects, they may be able to function as an invaluable resource for your team. The immutable fact in successful convergence environments is that they start slowly, with the honest and creative discussion of professionals from both sides of the aisle, and they build steam over time. You usually do not just converge an organization and many convergence tasks are not possible in some organizations, so it is often more about the exploration of enterprise risk within the organization and the search for solutions available within the skill sets and resources inherent to the business.

The second W is What, so it will be helpful to figure out exactly what you are going to converge. As discussed in Who, it might be helpful to acquire some outside expertise, at least for the planning phase, to help develop a core of ideas that might be feasible in your environment. Once the What component is worked out, you can begin to prioritize these projects and look for synergies between these options and other undertakings in the organization, and determine what the next best steps should be. This is an important activity because some of your projects might have impacts on other IT systems or business projects and you want to ensure that you minimize conflict and maximize leverage of other systems. For example, if you were considering a single-card solution for access control using a smart card, and you were going to need to link your systems with the business's existing directory services system, this might require a significant network architecture engagement as well. If the IT group is in the middle of a major IT system rollout and an external audit, this might not be the best time to suggest another complete rework of the network. However, if the facilities department is looking into building a new set of office towers, it might be an excellent time to suggest running CCTV systems across the data network instead of running a separate set of wires for the cameras.

The penultimate W is the Where, and this refers to which offices, departments, geographies, or other distinctive groups will be involved. If you are a small business, this might not be a major concern, but if you are a global conglomerate, this might certainly have an impact on your project scope and the composition of your team members.

The final W is When, and it relates to the prioritization and delivery of projects. It might be helpful to look at the When issues in the context of when you will want to be able to show results from your convergence projects. If there is an overarching enterprise risk management strategy project underway, you might want to dovetail your results within that report. If there are concerns across the organization for the protection of customer data, it might be the perfect time to announce a project that is helpful to this cause. In effect, I am saying that politics enters this discussion in many organizations, and if your project can be leveraged for complementary value you should consider that in your planning process. I was once faced with a rash of laptop thefts from some employee workspace areas, so I engaged a new program to use security guards to identify IT security risks at the desktop, which led to a complete halt of laptop thefts from these areas. Timing and packaging are everything!

## STEP 2. DATA GATHERING

A good start for any data-gathering phase of a project is to compile all relevant documents for the project team to examine. This is especially helpful during the brainstorming or creativity activities in your project planning phase. Policy manuals, risk assessments, contracts and legislation affecting the company, the company strategic plan, and even marketing documents are useful because there might be an opportunity to build interest in your project by linking your project goals to a larger initiative or business driver. If you help enable a strategic goal of the overall business, you are likely to get considerable support and funding for your project. If your project enables the business to make new claims regarding increased security levels or protection of customer information, this might become a strategic differentiator for the overall marketing program of the business. Any activity—whether it increases actual protection or reduces a perceived liability to industry legislation—will be helpful when considering convergence project options.

Another crucial data gathering activity is reviewing what others are doing in your industry, region, or the greater business world. You can gather a great deal of information by simply asking others what they are doing and finding out their lessons learned before you plunge deep into your projects. You can read industry journals and web sites, and attend conferences and professional development training to ensure that you have the requisite skills to take on the task. I have heard of organizations, such as Starbucks, that have attempted convergence and then de-converged after a period of time. Although I do not know the reasons for this, I can imagine the organizational change was quite a strain on those who were involved. Once you have gathered your internal and external information, you can begin to evaluate it for key pieces of information.

## STEP 3. INFORMATION ANALYSIS

One of the main outcomes of this analysis phase will be to understand what your vulnerabilities are in terms of the risk they represent to the business and how, potentially, new strategies can create value for the organization. It will be imperative to know where the hot points are and what the resistance arguments will be for your organization. Further, you may be able to gain some level of understanding of which echelon or depth of convergence will be right for your organization in the first stages of the project.

Your analysis might have qualitative and quantitative aspects, including trend analysis, security metrics review, and changes in the political and legislative environment, among many other characteristics. The specific goal of this stage is to provide a high level of assurance that you accurately understand the business drivers, conditions, and stakeholder needs before you attempt any organizational change. Although you may have a thorough grasp of this information if your organization is tightly contained, the larger or more decentralized the business is, the less likely it is that this may be the case.

## STEP 4. SOLUTION DESIGN

This is when you implement much of what is discussed in Chapter 13, and you focus on creating the framework for change. If you support the creeping incrementalism approach I discussed earlier, then the solution design phase will likely be well thought out and battle-tested on the front lines of your business. If you choose to try and implement convergence in a "big bang" approach, you might be perceived as radical or even enigmatic because many people might not understand the long-term vision and impact to them from the project. I am not saying this approach cannot work, because in some organizations it might be exactly what is needed.

## STEP 5. RECOMMENDATIONS

This part of the methodology is where you identify your conclusions from the analysis phase and develop your project recommendations and justifications. As previously stated, it will be helpful to link these recommendations to organizational objectives, measures, and overall strategy. If you can connect your project to the security value chain in your specific organization (as discussed in Chapter 24) and can identify how this recommendation will better protect the organization's core business activities, you will get additional support for the plan. This is also a great time to get your project sponsor sign-off on the plan, as you might soon need their help in building support for change.

## STEP 6. STAKEHOLDER EDUCATION SESSIONS

In some organizations it is best to start convergence projects with stakeholder education sessions, especially if there will be significant organizational change. If you are simply changing the routines of the security patrol staff, this will probably not be necessary; however, if you want to re-architect the entire data network, some preamble might be required. This might also give you an insight into any resistance you are going to encounter, and that might give you the opportunity to develop a strategy to overcome the resistance before it occurs (to the project's detriment).

## STEP 7. QUICK WINS

I will say this again because it is a key tool in your options for implementing convergence: If you start by picking off the low-hanging fruit and taking on easy-win projects, no matter how small, it will immutably start you off on the right foot with success and allow you to be seen as a leader who delivers value to the organization. In the organizations I have worked for, pilot projects have always been seen as lower risk than large-scale implementation of leading-edge ideas. This may work well for you, especially when seeking support for large, technical projects that present some risk to the IT environment.

## STEP 8. DO NOT GET MARRIED TO THE WHOLE IDEA OF CONVERGENCE

I believe that convergence is a menu, not an instruction booklet to be followed step-by-step to the end. You should take from it what works for you and your organization, and jettison everything else. Look for weaknesses and vulnerabilities in the way your enterprise security program works and seek to close those gaps, reduce the costs of delivering those services, and increase the knowledge of all security practitioners and executives in your organization.

## STEP 9. TRAINING

As a final word on the approach to the methodology of completing a convergence project, please remember that not all convergence can be accomplished with existing knowledge and skill sets. It is critical for long-term success that you cross-train your own staff through the process, have regular meetings so you can ease the tension and understand their fears, and ensure that their knowledge building is part of the success for the project. It might be helpful for them to know that during this training process you want them to generate ideas and make suggestions, because this is where the creativity comes from. Smart people focused on a task, sharing their knowledge and experience, is a positive, supportive environment.

# 17

## *Potential Benefits*

Numerous potential benefits are available from building converged security processes and adopting an enterprise-wide view for addressing security risk. Benefits can be categorized as originating from three broad categories: Risk factors, business process factors, and human factors. Risk factors can be defined as benefits that are delivered from risk mitigation, such as reduced liability, or increased compliance with governing legislation. Business process factors relate to benefits derived from cost savings, increased operational efficiency or business value, or reduction of the business process life cycle duration. Human factors can be described as benefits obtained from human interaction, including increased security awareness or improved morale or security department image and reputation. Although this is not an exhaustive list, many of the benefits will fit into one or more of these categories.

### RISK FACTORS

Risk factors could be best recognized by their contribution to the reduction of organizational security risk through a variety of mitigation strategies. Taken to the full extent of possible attributes, this could include activities such as programs that aid the organization in lowering potential liability exposures. An example of this might be through the creation of a converged risk assessment methodology that can be more frequently employed in both IT and physical applications. The converged risk assessment methodology evaluates both IT and physical issues in each application; therefore, risk is assessed more often and the potential exists to identify and mitigate vulnerabilities earlier.

Another risk mitigation outcome could be an increase in the organization's compliance level with industry legislation. Given the litany of penalties that can be imposed on businesses in both the public and private sectors around the world, this could be a tremendous asset to an organization, especially where the company's reputation is attached to its compliance record. A practical example of this would be an increased focus on the protection of personal information (as required under health care legislation, for example) by security patrol staff who are working closely with IT security professionals. Although protection of IT health care records is common practice in their electronic form, there is often less vigilance in protecting this information in their paper form. For example, some organizations are resistant to "clean desk" policies that require staff to put away their work at the day's end, or are lax in ensuring compliance to this policy. Security patrol staff who identify these risks can easily report breaches to the appropriate authority as part of their daily rounds, once they understand that this presents risk to the organization. Once the risks are identified, they can be mitigated before something ends up going out the door in the hands of a malicious janitor or tradesman.

One common attribute of converged security organizations is the delivery of cumulative security risk reports to senior management in a comprehensive or amalgamated form. When executives are fully informed about all security risks, they are better equipped to make the best possible decisions. A better-informed executive group might be inclined to approve extra security programs or allocate additional budget funds to security programs due to their fuller understanding of security risks. This can translate into lower risk, fewer incidents, or better compliance for the organization.

## BUSINESS PROCESS FACTORS

As previously alluded to, numerous items could be described as business process factors, including benefits derived from activities that produce cost savings or expense avoidance, increased efficiency or business value, or reduced cycle times in the business process. Cost savings, although a highly visible benefit, can come in many forms that are not always apparent, such as an *absence* of an expense or *avoidance* of a cost.

In our organization, it was common for physical security investigations to remain separate from IT security investigations. Inevitably, some physical security investigations would progress to having IT systems included in the scope, and the common practice was to outsource the forensic data work to a third party (which always came with a significant cost attached) to obtain this expertise. In our converged organization, the integrated investigation methodology leverages the existing technical skills inherent in the IT security group to perform the forensic review, bypassing the third-party vendor and saving thousands of dollars in the process. Although you could clearly label this benefit a cost savings or future cost avoidance, either way it immutably translates into true value to the business.

A more intricate example of cost savings or avoidance would be the decision to utilize the storage capacity of the network SAN in replacement of the purchase of future digital and network video recorders. In a large organization with buildings spread across a substantial geographical area, this could translate to tens or hundreds of thousands of dollars over a matter of just a few years, not to mention the increased operational reliability from having critical CCTV systems managed by the same management systems that typically deliver the 99.999% uptime that large network computer users are accustomed to receiving. As previously mentioned, although this solution will be not right for all organizations, many will be able to save on their existing budget by reducing ongoing maintenance costs of the video recorders and avoid future costs delivered from the lower price point of SAN storage versus DVR storage.

One of the more extraordinary cost avoidance options I have come across was related to the purchase of computer hardware. The primary operating platform at the present time for physical security systems is the PC or standard server. If you are a global organization that purchases large quantities of computers for physical security, you might already get a great deal on these devices. It will probably not be surprising to you that the IT groups of most organizations purchase many of these and are given steep volume discounts, and so your IT department might be able to reap this benefit as well. Your physical security vendor usually will sell you, at a significant markup, all the necessary hardware to work with the CCTV, access control, or alarm monitoring system that you purchase. I have personally seen vendors sell this equipment at a 50% profit margin over their cost of the hardware. If you purchase your hardware through your IT group at the greatly reduced price they can negotiate, and then have your vendor install its products on the hardware, you can save a tremendous amount of money over an extended period of time. Be aware that you might have some conflicts around warranty and maintenance of troublesome hardware items, but the money saved on the original purchase will easily finance some technician's time to address any problems. If you have purchased these computers through your own IT shop, they should also be supported by IT—obtaining antivirus, antispyware, patch updating, and a host of other protections from the IT group.

Just a quick word about my earlier comment regarding the increased efficiency and value delivered. In my role as IT security leader of our organization, I spent countless hours doing quarterly IT security policy compliance reviews at the desktop location. This meant that every 90 days my analyst and I would literally walk around to hundreds of desktops during the evening, looking for policy violations, such as unlocked laptops or passwords under the keyboard. Although this was both exhausting and organizationally rewarding, it was quite inefficient. Once we trained our corporate guard force to complete this function on a daily basis while they were on existing patrols, we benefited from the increased efficiency of my not performing the work and thereby being available to do other tasks. This also created more value for the organization in that risks were reduced by the guard staff. This reduction in my time involvement in the IT security policy compliance reviews freed me up to work on other tasks, such as IT security policy exception requests. This new free time allowed me to address these requests earlier and approve or seek clarification sooner, thereby shortening the cycle time needed to make administrative decisions and improving service to the business units.

Creating this new, converged organization provides an opportunity to engage some of the "sacred cows" of the security function. One somewhat vintage idea that still exists in many parts of the security industry is that security is a policelike function that follows a rigid command and control structure and is not concerned with customer service. In my experience, this has been common in large institutions such as campuses, government, or hospitals (these are just examples and are not meant to characterize these organizations at all; it has just been my experience). In organizations where I have come to work, I commonly issue an initial customer service survey to benchmark the level of concern with security and determine how the function is perceived. Although it has usually been good, it has not always been great. In my current organization, after engaging the security personnel in helping staff understand why they should be more aware of IT security issues at the desktop and at home, we saw a marked increase in customer satisfaction with the guard staff. It is a small issue, I grant you, but an important piece of the overall puzzle of security being recognized as part of the solution.

## HUMAN FACTORS

The final category of benefits is human factors, which is aptly named because of the relationship between human behavior and organizational security posture. I think it is nearly universally agreed that the human factor is the greatest unpredictable risk that confronts assets every day. In our organization, the changes we have instituted through combining "the geeks and the guards" to work together have led to significant organizational benefit. We have increased organizational security awareness across the business as a result of receiving constant support by the more aware and trained staff. The morale of our security staff is greatly enhanced, to the point of people making common reference to their appearance of increased happiness and professionalism. I attribute this to the security staff being actively involved in protecting the enterprise in a comprehensive manner and not being relegated to rattling doors for a living. Through these continual customer satisfaction surveys, the security group is perceived as a more professional and capable team by the staff and management of the organization. This position pays off in a multitude of ways—too many to catalog here. Also, the new training and integrated security programs have created new opportunities for leadership and professional development that drive the organizational learning quotient forward.

# 18

# *Security Convergence as Strategic Differentiator*

When discussing convergence or enterprise security risk, it is somewhat commonplace now to refer to it in the context of an enterprise using convergence to reduce risk, mitigate liability, and reduce costs. This brings to mind the question of how convergence can be useful for organizations that are vendors or service providers in the marketplace, on both sides of the former security industry divide. This chapter deals with the business strategy of strategic differentiation and how businesses can utilize convergence to differentiate themselves in new ways to drive new revenue opportunities, gain market share, and service customers in new ways.

Strategic differentiation can be defined as the "act of designing a set of meaningful differences to distinguish the company's offerings from the competitors' offerings."[1] This differentiation can take many forms, but most notably it involves providing a product or service that customers value in a location, at the time, for the price, or at the volume that separates it from its competitors. This distinction entices customers to purchase from the differentiating entity rather than from its competitors. Now this is hardly a new concept and you see it every day, but astute business tacticians will recognize the evolution of convergence as an opportunity to differentiate a host of businesses in the security industry.

Let us start by selecting a typical mid-sized security company in a medium-sized market, a sprawling urban environment of 3 million people. This company's portfolio of services includes security guard and mobile patrol, an alarm systems division, and security consulting services. They are mid-priced providers—they are not generally the most expensive company in their market but also not the cheapest. On average, in this market, this firm will probably sell essentially the same services as most other companies in the market and will have to compete on either price, quality, or image to increase its market share. It has no real way to differentiate itself, other than making claims that it is better for one reason or another, which is often difficult to substantiate given the cost structure of the industry.

This cost structure is in place because the industry is essentially commoditized with little radical innovation, and customers have become educated about the products and services. This education has enabled them to negotiate lower rates and better deals, putting financial pressure on the industry to cut costs and focus on core competencies and services to maintain profit margins. We see examples of this in everyday life, but I will use an example I recently have seen. Laser eye surgery used to cost thousands of dollars per eye because the market would bear this cost, given that no one understood how the service worked—they just "saw" the results. As the service became more common with new technology and service providers entering the marketplace, the cost has steadily come down to the point where now it is literally 20% of what it cost five years ago. Now that the customer is educated and has many choices, the price has trended down. This is nothing more than the reality of macroeconomic supply and demand.

Now, what if we inserted a new set of services into our security company example, which were specialized, offered by no one else, and provided substantial value to the customer? This company might be able to justify higher rates because of this increased specialization, or it might just be able to make a new argument as to why it should be chosen over a competitor as the service provider for a particular customer.

To address specific strategies for a firm to differentiate itself, let us return to previous chapters. I spoke about how, for the City of Vancouver, we used our corporate guard force to patrol buildings and identify IT security risks. This was done through minimal training. When I have spoken to others about this, they told me that they would love this service but they have contract security personnel, and training them (given their staff turnover) makes this problematic. If a security company took the time to understand a customer's problems, it might recognize that an opportunity exists to add a training component to the initial mandatory guard training to deliver this service to the customer. Imagine the value to a customer if its guard company could identify an unlocked laptop ripe to be stolen, a rogue wireless router hidden under a desk (against policy), or a wiring closet left open by a contractor, which exposes a sensitive server? This value created would certainly differentiate this company from all other guard companies in the industry.

When looking at the security systems division of this company, it is logical to suggest that when selling computer-based equipment to a customer, such as CCTV and access control systems, it would be reasonable to ensure that the customer is aware of the risks to the equipment from the customer's own IT environment. It also follows that the environment that the equipment will operate in, such as the corporate data network, faces threats both externally and internally and that these threats create risks to the new security systems. Given the converging threats of IT and physical security systems (their common reliance on the data network and their common risks related to the Internet and malicious software), it would be a great opportunity for physical security systems companies to understand more fully the risks these systems face. At the very least, they should ensure that their customers fully appreciate the risks they are accepting or know what they should do to investigate potential risks to their environment related to this equipment. Far too often I have seen companies install equipment with little more than simple configuration of the purchased applications and rudimentary testing, and then they move on. For the technically unsophisticated consumer, such as residential condominium environments, community centers, and small businesses that cannot afford security expertise in-house, this does the customer a significant disservice and translates into a massive missed opportunity to educate the customer and build longer-term loyalty.

Now let us look at this from the point of view of an IT security consultant in that same marketplace. This will be especially relevant if you are located in a jurisdiction where physical security professionals are required to be licensed by a government authority to practice security consulting. IT security practitioners often get involved in projects designing security controls for organizations or conducting risk assessments of customers' IT infrastructures. Inevitably, there are physical security aspects to these assessments or design engagements, and the IT practitioner is faced with either bringing in outside resources to add creditability, or be in compliance with jurisdictional licensing legislation, for their physical security recommendations. IT security practitioners can differentiate themselves to their customers by becoming certified in physical security disciplines, such as the Certified Protection Professional (CPP) or Physical Security Professional (PSP) designations through ASIS International, or by ensuring that they have those resources on staff to identify their firm as a full service enterprise security consultant. Although I have not yet seen any firms positioning themselves this way, it is only a matter of time before someone integrates this skill set into their product mix and separates themselves from the congregation of competitors.

The previous two examples dealt strictly with private sector enterprises, but even government can benefit from convergence and differentiation. Although strategic differentiation is the last thing you would think government leadership would have on its collective mind, you may be surprised at the extent to which collective reputation plays into the opinions people hold about an organization or a region.

Businesses make the decision to locate their operations in jurisdictions for many reasons, including the perception that the government is competent and will respond to their needs. Political leaders are often judged by the actions or inactions of the staff in their departments. Public-facing organizations are always trying to compare themselves to similar organizations and show how they are thought to be leading or governing in a prudent manner. These issues and many others are motivation to ensure that all reasonable opportunities to minimize costs, increase risk mitigation, and efficiently utilize resources are leveraged.

## REFERENCE

1. Kotler, P. *Marketing Management*, 10th ed. Upper Saddle River, NJ: Prentice Hall, p. 284.

# 19

## The Human Resources Perspective

### MEETING THE HUMAN RESOURCE CHALLENGES OF A CONVERGED ORGANIZATION

With the challenge of achieving security convergence comes the accompanying challenge of ensuring that people—and people practices—are equal to the task. Without insight into the very specific and demanding human resources (HR) requirements of such an initiative, the end result is almost certain to be compromised and the drive for change effectively undermined.

In this chapter, I aim to look at the human resource challenges from the perspective of an organization about to embark upon security convergence. However, I believe that these observations are equally applicable to other environments at varying stages of implementation. [At the end of the chapter, I will consider the individual perspectives of a number of interested parties, from a CSO about to undertake a converged role to an HR practitioner tasked with finding a suitable candidate.]

Before embarking upon such an endeavor, it is important that all readers, irrespective of their standpoint, appreciate the following:

- True security convergence of physical and IT security requires a leader who possesses the appropriate talent, ability, and experience.
- Because only a limited number of organizations have—so far—converged their IT and physical security operations, there are still relatively few individuals with hands-on experience of leading security convergence.

This is not to say that convergence cannot be undertaken without such an individual already in place to guide the process. However, having such a person will increase the chances of success and the likelihood that the benefits of convergence are maximized and appreciated by all, so it is important to ensure that the correct skill sets are in place. Of course, the simple way to achieve this is to recruit an individual with the appropriate crossover of skills—ideally one who has a track record of successfully converging an organization similar to your own! But in the short term, this might prove problematic and the answer could be to "grow your own," identifying the most likely candidates (internal or external) with the capability to learn and to grow. I will return to this when I deal with CSO recruitment but, for now, suffice it to say that vision, ability, and determination might be the best combination upon which to build.

From an HR perspective, there are a number of specific challenges to navigating this new world. No matter what the environment (corporate, commercial, governmental, or any other) there are new threats, new demands, and new business drivers and an imperative to respond in order to survive and prosper, as well as to meet the appropriate legislative or governance challenges. Whether it is a need to meet the dictates of corporate governance, such as the Sarbanes-Oxley Act, or the commercial imperative to protect proprietary information, or simply the need to maximize internal efficiencies, the journey remains remarkably similar.

Before embarking on security convergence, one must understand both the price of success and the cost of failure because they impact both the business and the human resources of the organization. Just as success can mean more than simply safeguarding important proprietary information, it can also mean gaining an edge over competitors and increasing market share. Similarly, failure can be a lot more than just another change management initiative that becomes derailed; it can conceivably lead to legislative action by the authorities or even to commercial ruin.

We cannot underestimate the considerable impact that security convergence will have on the people in the organization:

- On senior management, to whom convergence might need to be sold; who might be called upon champion it; and who, whether they realize it or not, will have a vested interest in its success or failure.
- On HR staff, who might be tasked with finding and training the people who will make this happen and with helping to identify the processes that make it live or die.
- On security personnel themselves, who might welcome it or resist it; who might see it as logical change, enhancing their own roles and career opportunities; or who might see it as a threat to their comfort zones or even their jobs; and who have the power to undermine it or help it achieve its full potential.
- On all staff within the organization, whose working lives are potentially impacted by such change; whose resistance can be yet one more barrier to effective implementation; or whose acceptance of this change will help to ensure its ongoing success.

## THE "CONVERGED CHIEF SECURITY OFFICER"

For the purposes of this book, the "converged CSO" is the CSO with the hands-on experience and skills to effectively implement and run a fully converged security operation. Although, as observed above, such a person is still relatively rare, this is rapidly changing as organizations—and security professionals—respond to the need for the vision and the skill sets that can make security convergence a reality. These individuals are aggressively pursuing the training and qualifications required to succeed in this new world.

## The Leadership Qualities

The converged CSO is an individual who, in addition to having many other qualities, embodies the following:

- Is a leader rather than a manager.
- Possesses vision.
- Understands the necessity of selling the idea of convergence at all levels throughout the organization.
- Can build commitment, communicate the rationale for change, and drive that change to successful implementation.
- Understands that, irrespective of environment or goals, everything connects to operating efficiencies, risk mitigation, and, where appropriate, the bottom line.

That description might categorize a number of senior leaders in a diverse range of functions. Beyond that, the converged CSO is someone who not only understands the differences between the physical and IT security functions but, more importantly, the similarities and the benefits that can accrue from their convergence.

## Understanding and Supporting the Role

From the perspective of any CEO or HR professional attempting to clarify a strategic overview of the converged CSO's role, it is vitally important that they understand not just the purpose of that role but also the rationale underlying the need for strategic change itself. As with all change management scenarios, the reason for the proposed change needs to be clearly understood by all involved. This involves clear communication lines and messaging at all levels throughout the organization.

There needs to be clarity regarding how the objective of security convergence matches corporate and organizational objectives and how it will ultimately enhance operational efficiency and the bottom line. Where there are potential staffing implications, this needs to be handled with the usual sensitivity, remembering that not everyone might see an extension of their role as a benefit!

## Reporting Lines

Where existing functions are to be combined, there is a strong need to clarify duties and responsibilities as well as identify reporting lines. Who will report to whom within the new regime? What is the rationale for this and has it been well explained and communicated?

And to whom will the CSO report? It will not be the traditional route for Security (such as for Facilities or Operations), nor the usual route for IT, within the IT department itself. The appointment itself should ideally be at the chief officer level, as this reflects the central importance of the function. If not personally a member of the "top table," the appointee needs to report to a member of the Board, ideally the CEO or a senior member of the audit management team. In any event, it should be clear who this is and that they will, in turn, need to understand that they must champion the newly created function.

Along with seniority comes the question of what budgetary control accompanies the new role. There is little substitute for controlling the funds that allow one to make the strategic and operational decisions required for service delivery. Whether or not the role is represented at the most senior levels, an organization should nevertheless consider to what extent budgetary control and decision-making authority should be devolved to the CSO.

## Defining Job Descriptions

As with any role, regardless of seniority, there is a need to identify not just the purpose and primary role of the job but also the specific responsibilities of the position in question. With a new role it is important to ensure that a certain flexibility exists. All job descriptions are fluid in the sense that they mutate over time to meet the changing needs of the function and of the organization, but clarity of purpose, supported by detail, will ensure that appointees have the requisite comfort at a time of transition.

With respect to the CSO's position and that of other management roles, it is important to elicit the input of the appointee(s) who will understand better than anyone the demands of their new role(s). This will allow HR professionals to compile job descriptions at all levels that appropriately reflect the reality of the new world. How much detail should be provided will largely be dictated by how much detail is possessed by the subject matter expert in the field—the converged CSO.

## RECRUITING AND SELECTING THE RIGHT CHIEF SECURITY OFFICER

Whether undertaken by a CEO, a senior manager, an HR professional within an organization, or a consultant tasked with recruitment, the recruitment process itself is largely the same. In addition to understanding the basics of how to handle any search and selection process, you will need to know the following:

- The most likely places to look for—and find—talented and qualified CSO candidates; how to draft and place an advertisement that encapsulates the challenges of the role and summarizes the likely qualifications and experience required.
- Where to place such an ad so that it reaches the right demographic and/or specialist management groups.
- If engaging a search firm, how to brief the agency, ensuring that you are clear on your needs. Many search firms have valuable expertise in certain areas, so make sure that they truly understand the philosophy behind security convergence and are cognizant of the challenges implicit in making it work; only then will they be properly equipped to try and identify appropriate candidates. Where possible, you should consider engaging a specialist with a strong understanding of the CSO function.
- If internal candidates apply (especially those in existing physical or IT security roles), you will need to consider how best to handle these applicants and how best to assess their expertise and their likely success in the role. In the event that you decide to appoint an external candidate, you should consider how this appointment should be handled with respect to the unsuccessful internal applicants—what feedback should be provided, what development options should be considered or offered, and how you will, in effect, keep these valuable staff members on-side if they remain in the organization.

    The assessment process will need to be handled with great care, especially with respect to a role that is new to the organization. You will need to ensure that the skill sets you want to assess are indeed indicative of success in the role and that the qualifications required (or desired) are relevant to the respective functions within the role. Until such time as specific qualifications are introduced that certify the knowledge base required to become an effective CSO in a converged security environment, perhaps a combination of qualifications should be considered. These could include the Certified Protection Professional (CPP), the Physical Security Professional (PSP), the Certified Information Systems Security Professional (CISSP), and the Certified Information Security Manager (CISM) certifications. (I will return to these designations later in this chapter.)

- As is always the case in any recruitment process (but is so often overlooked), there is a need for recruiters to sell "the organization." It is not just the candidate who should be presenting his or her best face; it remains vitally important for the organization to offer an honest assessment of the current status of its security operations. If you believe that the CSO role is not yet fully defined in your organization, it is important to unequivocally state this during the interview process. If the appointee will be required to assist in further defining the CSO role, this should be made clear. If you need to find a self-starter, then make sure that this requirement emerges at interview. In a perfect world, the chosen candidate will be a partner in establishing the CSO role. The worst result for everyone would be a mismatch between the expectations of the organization and candidate, and the reality on the ground.

## Reviewing Qualifications

In the preceding section I refer to the current qualifications that might be indicative of the knowledge base required to succeed in a CSO's role:

- CPP: Certified Protection Professional (ASIS International)
- PSP: Physical Security Professional (ASIS International)

- CISSP: Certified Information Systems Security Professional (ISC)
- CISM: Certified Information Security Manager (Information Systems Audit and Control Association)

These certifications can offer employers a comfort level that a candidate's knowledge base is sufficient to meet at least some of the requirements of a Converged CSO's role.

## The Interviews

Assuming that your organization is seeking a CSO to lead a converged security function, how should the interview be handled? The following questions need to be asked:

- Who should interview? How senior should they be? This will, to some extent, depend upon the respective seniority accorded to the converged role; however, the final approval needs to be at the most senior level possible—and almost certainly a senior executive at the Board level. Initial short-listing interviews may be handled at a lower level in the organization (ideally with the support of professional HR staff), but it is vital that all interviewers, at all levels and phases in the process, understand the nature of the role and the rationale underlying not just the appointment but also the decision to converge the security functions.
- What to ask, and how? Given the unique nature of the function and the possibility that some candidates will not possess a strong track record of working within a converged function, it will be important for interviewers to ensure that situational questions are featured prominently in order to provide a likely predictor of the candidate's approach if they are selected. In addition to displaying a solid understanding of the benefits of convergence, interviewers would be well advised to seek a sophisticated appreciation of the difficulties implicit in such an initiative as well as a realistic overview of the challenges the appointee and his or her team could face.

- There is no ideal profile for a CSO, but the challenges of establishing, running, and developing the function mean that a number of key skills are demanded. It is important to remember that the viability of the converged function depends upon its ability to improve performance, enhance efficiency, and improve the bottom line. To this end, it is unlikely that a CSO appointee would succeed unless he or she demonstrated competence in being able to itemize these benefits, and were compelling in being able to "sell" ongoing commitment to the initiative. Communication and presentational skills will be highly important. To succeed, a CSO will need to be compelling at the top table, whether visiting or in residence there.
- In addition to the hard data of educational and professional credentials, hands-on experience in either or both physical and IT security is essential. My purpose here is not to suggest a likely profile for the converged CSO, but to highlight the importance of candidates understanding—and possessing—the skills it takes to succeed in such a demanding role.

## The Appropriateness of Testing

"To Test or Not to Test": that is the question. In discussing this, I need to differentiate between ability testing and the taking of a so-called personality inventory. The former can provide some insight into hard skills (such as vocabulary, literacy, or attention to detail), and some situational testing (such as "in-tray" exercises) can have much to offer in terms of additional insight. But the personality inventory, when used appropriately and correctly, and in conjunction with an in-depth interview conducted by a skilled practitioner, can predict likely working styles and behavior in the workplace. Given the right inventories and the right environment, it could also look at the likely fit with the corporate management team. For a Board-level appointment, this could be an important and useful tool. Each organization will decide what is right for it and for its environment, but these are all potentially useful tools which, in the right hands, can provide further assurance to recruiters.

## The Other Side of the Coin: What the Right CSO Candidate Is Likely to Be Seeking

Increasingly, a CSO in a converged environment is well aware of his or her value to an organization, which might be dependent on the ability to stay ahead of the curve and remain commercially competitive and operationally sharp. Accordingly, it is important for those tasked with recruitment to be aware of the following factors that are likely to be of importance to CSO candidates of the right caliber:

- *Organizational status.* This is extremely important because the success or ultimate failure of the converged function might depend upon the seniority of the individual in the driving seat. A presence in, or access to, the Board Room will be vital and, for some candidates, this will be a determinant of whether the job is appropriately attractive. Organizations should be able to demonstrate that the role has been accorded the requisite seniority. Similarly, reporting lines (both above and below) should reflect the importance of the function to the organization.
- *Degrees of autonomy and freedom.* This runs in tandem with seniority and is, as much as anything, an indicator of the senior-level commitment to the convergence initiative. Although one might reasonably expect the degree of one's eventual autonomy within an organization to be based upon one's own credibility, any suggestion that the resources required to effectively direct matters might not be readily available to the appointee will send warning signals that senior management might be less than totally supportive of the convergence initiative.
- *Ability to make strategy and policy.* With autonomy come a number of benefits, all of which can have a direct impact on organizational effectiveness. The ability to set strategy and make policy—often on an enterprise-wide basis—is a clear indicator of the importance accorded not just to the CSO but to the converged security function. Although no discipline can function in a vacuum, the ability to devise and implement effective and timely policies is of special

importance in a dynamic, changing function such as converged security. The very nature of emergent IT security threats underlines the need for an organization to respond swiftly. If it cannot do so within its existing policy framework, then this needs to be quickly remedied. An inability to easily achieve this (perhaps as a result of bureaucratic process) is likely to be a strong negative indicator to a potential CSO.

- *Professional qualifications.* Although not always indicative of ability in a role, professional qualifications do provide both comfort and credibility—comfort that the candidate possesses the requisite specialist knowledge as it relates to the professional function, and credibility at all levels with respect to the knowledge they can bring to the table. The strong candidate will possess far more than simple certifications, but their importance (such as a strong educational background) should not be underestimated. The possession of suitable qualifications will very likely have an impact on the marketability, and therefore the price, of a good candidate.

- *Compensation and benefits.* Last, but clearly not least to the appointee, is "The Package." The pay of CSOs has risen dramatically in the last few years, as the role they play in any effectively managed organization has become increasingly important. With the advent of convergence, this level has only increased further, recognizing the unique experience, qualifications, and skill sets required of post-holders. The elevation of the function has seen the installation of many CSOs at the most senior management levels, and salary packages reflect this. As with all disciplines, it is possible to hire for less, but there are often consequences to this—not just for the function but for the organization itself. I am not advocating ever-escalating pay levels for the converged CSO, but I am stressing the importance of ensuring that, as with all functions, your organization's remuneration policy is cognizant of current market rates. The old adage remains true: You get what you pay for.

So what will the Converged CSO be seeking from an employer? For the right people, there are obviously intellectual and operational challenges on this new frontier, but employers should understand that opportunity alone is insufficient. Such expertise has a price that is dictated by a market increasingly aware of the expertise and experience that the converged CSO can bring to the table.

## BUILDING THE CONVERGED SECURITY DEPARTMENT

Assuming that a CSO is already in place and that the strategy for convergence has been defined, the key question is: Where do we go next? My purpose here is not to provide an exhaustive checklist of how to proceed (all organizations are unique, have different needs, and are at different stages of development), but simply to identify a number of key initiatives that will need to be addressed by all entities engaged in this process.

## Training and Development

Although this might seem to be an initiative more focused on the newly converged security department and its staff, there is a broader, ongoing need to be met. Obviously, individuals previously functioning within either the physical or IT security departments will need significant knowledge to appreciate the duties undertaken by their colleagues and to address their changed roles, and there is a broader requirement for staff across the organization to understand the changed environment.

Internally, one might initially undertake a training needs analysis on the newly converged department, identifying the skill sets required to effectively perform the new functions and assessing any skill gap between these and the existing staff competencies. Specific training programs could be designed to ensure a cross-fertilization of the respective skill sets of physical and IT security staff. In almost all cases, IT security staff are unfamiliar with the discipline and dictates of physical security (from access control to CCTV), and physical security staff are unaware of the many and diverse elements of protecting the network. And although patrol staff are unlikely to become responsible for patching the network any time soon, it is entirely possible that as part of their regular patrol duties they could easily be required to identify a variety of workstation security lapses or even sniff out unauthorized wireless hotspots.

As in all senior-level appointments, it is appropriate to review what training or learning needs a newly appointed CSO has. These could relate to more than the learning curve presented by a new environment, although this will be obviously be dependent upon the skill set and experience possessed by the appointee.

What about other senior Board-level and senior management staff? What do they need to know about the new converged direction? Naturally, it is vital that all senior personnel share in the buy-in if the benefits of security convergence are to be maximized. It should not be assumed that the rationale and the benefits of convergence are evident for all to see. Accordingly, a program of awareness and education should be adopted at all levels within the organization with content appropriate for each audience, dependent on their involvement, seniority, and current familiarity with the function. For example, a Board-level presentation is more likely to focus on governance systems and enterprise-wide benefits and offer far more detail than a communiqué prepared for front-line staff. Those individuals or departments with a deeper involvement might require more specific and detailed programs. As convergence progresses, it might also become necessary to communicate ongoing changes such as new policies and/or procedures, and this will need to be done in a way that clearly and effectively explains the rationale for such change.

One important question that a converged organization—and its CSO—needs to ask is: What training will be needed to grow the next generation of leadership? This is still a relatively new discipline and it is therefore incumbent upon today's leaders to ensure that the expertise and experience required to develop and grow the function (both within the organization and more generally) are carefully nurtured. One possible danger can exist when an organization embraces convergence and implements change, driven by a talented and visionary security professional. Then, regardless of the initiatives adopted and the progress made, if there is no attempt to share that expertise with others within the organization, the entire convergence model is in danger of collapse should that individual leave. This highlights the need to sell the benefits of such an initiative at the highest level and devote ongoing resources to ensuring that staff development is not limited to the skills specific to individual job functions. A broader knowledge of convergence and its benefits will be required if these vital change management initiatives are not to be derailed. In this respect, a CSO in a newly converged organization has a vital role to play in developing the next generation of talent. Whether as coach, mentor, or simply an enabler, he or she must build the foundations of future success by investing in the next generation of converged security professionals.

## Succession Planning and Management

The identification of critical positions within any organizational function is a discipline that pays benefits in many areas, from business continuity to manpower planning. In light of the observations above, this is especially critical where a converged security operation is concerned. Traditionally, one might expect to undertake a full, two-year program of succession planning before expecting any significant payoff. However, the prediction of manpower needs is far from an exact science and is impacted by many external forces over which we have little or no control. This imprecision and difficulty should not deter us from approaching this in a methodical and meticulous fashion.

The identification of internal staff who have the potential to move higher up in the organization (whether simply identified as possessing above-average competence or clearly tagged as "stars") presents us with the question of what we are then going to do about it. The identification of this talent may happen in a number of ways, some formal and some informal, but the individuals in question are likely to emerge from the workforce or, in the case of fast-track recruitment, be identified for enhanced development at the hiring stage.

To maximize the chances of success, a dedicated budget should be established for succession planning. This inevitably will have some crossover with the training budget, but could well feature funding for development courses without immediate (or even obvious) operational payback. In addition to management development initiatives, such courses could include strategic planning, policy making, or even financial management.

In a perfect world, these future leaders would receive the training, development, and support they need to take the organization forward into the future. Appropriate senior roles would emerge and they would take up the reins and return the organization's (substantial) investment through performance, competence, and continuity. Again, this is an inexact science and the unpredictable has an alarming tendency to occur. One thing is clear, however: The best chance of maintaining an efficient, forward-thinking, converged security department lies in investing in your people.

## Retention

Retention is a key initiative that all organizations need to address. This is even more acute in a demanding and emerging market where talent and expertise are scarce. Staff turnover is both natural and healthy but, when unmanaged, can have an enormous impact on operational efficiency. Discontinuity of people and knowledge has the potential to undermine even the best-organized environment. In contract guarding, for example, the inability of many firms to retain quality guards has a seriously detrimental impact on service continuity and is the single most important factor in service breakdown and lost contracts.

Within a corporate environment, the impact of poor retention can be similarly problematic. There is no magic formula for staff retention but a number of measures can be undertaken to understand trends and prepare for, and respond to, potential difficulties. It is therefore important to identify and monitor security department turnover in order to compare this data against that available on market trends. Should departmental voluntary turnover levels be significantly above or below industry norms, it is important to understand why and, in the case of the former, determine remedial measures to attempt to rectify the situation. Of course, data alone will not reveal the reasons for any such disparity, so it is important to understand how the situation in which staff find themselves impacts their respective decisions to stay or go. In the case of departing staff, it is not helpful to assume that one understands all the factors involved in the decision to leave; in this respect, the exit interview can prove invaluable. This structured interview (ideally conducted by someone at arm's length from the staff member in question—most likely the HR department) seeks to ascertain, in a friendly and open exchange, all the factors that might be involved in a staff member's decision to leave. Such a decision could be based on a simple, single factor (such as the relocation of a partner), but it could also reveal a number of organizational or departmental issues previously unknown or unaddressed.

An important element in retention planning is attempting to benchmark the organization's compensation and benefits to ensure that these are in line with industry norms. In any new discipline, such as converged security, this will require research. It might be necessary to subscribe to the latest salary surveys in order to track such information. The questions, of course, are what action one takes to counter any disparity and how swiftly such remedial measures can be put in place. In organizations with integrated job evaluation programs, creativity might be required to respond in a timely and effective fashion without creating organization-wide discrepancies and dangerous precedents!

On a broader level, questions should also be asked about staff perceptions of the organization and even the department. Do they understand its purpose? Do they support it? Do they share in and relate to its values? My purpose here is not to suggest that organizations immediately embark on costly communication surveys or adopt employment branding initiatives (although all of these may have a place in increasing understanding and in building morale and purpose). Rather, managers should look beneath the surface when assessing the complex issue of staff retention.

## Communication and Orientation

Communication is, of course, far more than the corporate initiative referred to above. It underlies every aspect of our working lives. It is fundamental to success or failure in all spheres, especially in new undertakings which might be met with misunderstanding, mistrust, or even outright suspicion (including, of course, a converged security operation).

There are a number of avenues open to organizations seeking to enhance communication with their employees, especially regarding new and important enterprise-wide initiatives. Key to the ongoing success of a converged security operation is the establishment and communication of the corporate message to all staff, once again sharing the rationale for and the importance of security in every aspect of their working lives. The framing and the level of detail might be different depending on the audience, but the key message will remain the same. This will need to be communicated to all staff, whether existing or newly joined, within the security department or within the wider organization. And there will be an ongoing need for reinforcement as time progresses. Again, this will need to be carefully framed in order to avoid message overload and to avoid the reaction from staff that they have "heard it all before." Consideration could be given to finding some organizational communication forum to regularly communicate with staff regarding various aspects of security awareness and good practice. Examples of such venues could range from corporate newsletters to notice boards and the organization's intranet.

Finally, we should not overlook the induction and orientation of the new CSO. Whether the organization is already converged or is embarking on the road to convergence, it will be important that the new appointee understands the nature of the organization and the details of its enterprise-wide approach to risk, in the shortest possible time. All pertinent information should be made available and a structured orientation program should be devised, ideally in conjunction with the appointee, ensuring that all of his or her needs are met. A carefully planned orientation and induction program should help ensure that a new CSO, irrespective of background, should be well positioned to contribute as soon as possible. The seemingly obligatory requirement to "hit the ground running" should provide added impetus to this undertaking!

## Performance Management

Finally, one needs to look at how we determine the performance in the CSO role of the new appointee and, in due course, that of the department. In a newly converged environment, the old performance measures are unlikely to be adequate to evaluate the delivery of departmental objectives. Indeed, those very objectives have probably changed.

First, there is likely to be a need to reevaluate security and risk management objectives on an enterprise-wide basis. Only after this exercise can appropriate departmental objectives be established, consistent with corporate goals. These objectives need to be understood by all involved in their delivery, no matter how peripheral or incidental. They might well be challenging but they need to remain achievable in order to maintain staff buy-in. They also need to be reviewed on a regular basis, not just for compliance but also in terms of their ongoing appropriateness in a dynamic and ever-changing environment. The regularity of reviews needs to be established, as do the suitability and the mechanics of the measurement system, from key performance indicators to the methods of data capture.

Whether or not such a system is applied to the performance of the organization, to the security department, to the CSO and his or her staff, or to all of these, it is important that the twin issues of recognition and reward are carefully addressed. Success should be observed and rewarded, either through individual or group bonuses, profit-sharing or gain-sharing mechanisms, or simple recognition and awards.

## DIFFERENT PERSPECTIVES, DIFFERENT QUESTIONS

The perspective of each reader (from CEO to HR manager to consultant, and so on) will undoubtedly differ in major ways, but the following section identifies a number of areas that you will inevitably need to address when considering the converged security environment and your own role (whatever that may be) in creating it, staffing it, running it and, of course, succeeding in it.

## For HR Professionals

As an HR professional in a security converged organization, you might be tasked with recruiting, retaining, and even training the talent required to deliver the vision articulated by senior management. These are some of the questions you need to ask:

- Do you have senior management buy-in for recruiting at the appropriate level? Who will be your client on this assignment? The CEO?

- The people are out there, but where do you look? Which industry bodies (e.g., the Alliance for Enterprise Security Risk Management, ASIS, ISSA, ISACA), publications (e.g., *Security Management*, *CSO Magazine*), or specialist sites do you need to explore?
- What is the right background for the job in question? What is the right skill set? The right experience? Once you have established these criteria, how do you propose to validate them?
- What is the job description for the new role? Does it exist? If not, who will establish it? If you are required to write it, do you possess sufficient understanding?
- How do you establish the market rate for such a leader?
- What is the current state of convergence in your organization? How much start-up expertise will a suitable candidate require? How will you determine whether he or she is a self-starter?
- If the job brief involves actually converging the function, does the candidate have the people skills to achieve this without alienating staff?
- If convergence requires recruiting new talent, how do you keep the existing staff on-side, especially those who might feel they are being overlooked?

## For CSO Candidates

- Do you understand the nature of the environment to which you are applying? Does the organization appear to be truly committed to convergence?
- To what level does this role report? What autonomy will it offer you? What budgetary control? Does it seem sufficient to ensure success? If not, what else should you be seeking?
- Do you know your market value? Is the salary range and package being offered appropriate for the role and the size of the organization? Do any bonuses in the offer appear achievable?
- Do you have a realistic understanding of the challenges implicit in such a role?

- Have you undertaken an inventory of your strengths and weaknesses as a leader in a converged role? What are you doing to address any concerns or shortfalls that might exist?
- What would your training and/or development needs be if appointed? What (if any) additional qualifications should you be considering? Will these improve your knowledge base and/or your marketability?
- If you were to be appointed, how would you begin your task?

## For CEOs

- Do you understand how a converged security operation fits into an enterprise-wide approach to risk?
- If convergence is not already implemented, are you and the top team truly committed to security convergence? Do you have a realistic understanding of the challenges, benefits, and costs implicit in such an initiative?
- To whom will the CSO report? Is this consistent with the stated commitment?
- Do you and your HR staff have a realistic understanding of remuneration levels for a CSO in your industry and in an organization of your size?

## For Consultants

- Does your client have a realistic understanding of what you will (and will not) be providing, be it a strategic outline for security convergence, an action plan for implementation, or assistance in the search for a new CSO?
- Does the client understand the implications of converged security on an enterprise level?
- If you are only providing a piece of the convergence jigsaw puzzle, are you able to advise your client on how to proceed with the next step(s)?
- Has the purpose of your assignment been sufficiently well communicated to those who need to know? How will you establish this and what measures will you take to address any failures?

- How are you likely to be viewed by the existing security staff, whether physical or IT? Will this have an impact on delivery?

## For Existing Staff in Both Physical and IT Security

- Do you understand how convergence will impact your current role and duties?
- What do you need to know about the process to enable you to better contribute?
- What are your learning needs? Do you currently have skill gaps?
- What specific training courses, qualifications, and/or certifications would best help you in this converged world? Will your employer pay for these?
- What opportunities can convergence present in terms of advancement and/or job enrichment?
- What long-term career prospects might now exist that were not there previously? If any of these interest you, what do you need to do to learn more and position yourself appropriately?

# *Sustainability*

# Integrated Threat and Event Reporting

## 20

The basic premise of this chapter is that a better-informed executive team can make more prudent decisions. I do not think I am taking a big leap here by putting a stake in the ground and claiming that management staff who are informed about *all* of the enterprise risk in a cumulative fashion are better informed than if they get this information in a more fragmented manner. Metrics, event reports, and key performance indicators all approximate the activity and relative performance of a business activity or the business overall. If the popular management dictum of "What gets measured, gets done" is true, then measuring security performance and the rate of incidents is crucial in terms of moving forward the asset protection strategies of the business.

Security metrics essentially measure activity-based characteristics of an organization and can generally be categorized as process-oriented or outcome-oriented. Process-oriented metrics track the performance of a process, such as the number or percentage of employees who received a security orientation at the time of being hired by the organization. This metric will tell you the effectiveness of policy and procedures. If, as in this example, business units are required by policy to ensure that new hires receive a security orientation but only 75% of employees have received the briefing, obviously, this will be an indicator of problems in policy compliance or security awareness at the supervisor, HR, or management level.

Outcome-oriented metrics will measure the end results of a characteristic, such as the total downtime of a network or system. This type of metric will represent the robustness of the item being measured. For example, if your firewall or e-mail server is down 3% of the time during business hours because of virus attacks, this would be an indication of a serious need to improve the antivirus program at your organization.

Metrics should identify factors that are crucial to the business; they should be carefully set up to not measure extraneous activity. Given a finite set of resources, issues that are essential to the business should be the focal point of the metrics program. It is easy to get drawn into measuring every detail of an organization's performance, but the items measured must add value—especially if this is for the purpose of reporting to senior management.

Security function key performance indicators (KPIs) elucidate the relative performance of the security function across the organization. Metrics track the incident behavior, whereas KPIs track the performance of the security function. Common KPIs can include the number of dollars per employee spent on security during the year or the percentage of the organization's total budget spent on security. Other KPIs can relate to performance of staff functions, such as the number of security awareness sessions delivered per month or the number of vulnerability scans of the data network performed annually. KPIs can also be customer service-driven, such as the average number of days needed to review and resolve policy exception requests or the percentage of security incidents reported versus total incidents known by security.

Metrics and KPIs tell the security story and identify the organization's relative risk posture. When these characteristics are tracked and trended over a number of years, they provide a basis for comparison on a continuous scale and can become a powerful management tool and a basis for future business cases.

In an environment where security groups are independent of each other and report to senior management through discrete channels, it is nearly impossible for any organization to fully appreciate the intricacies of the security posture the enterprise faces. Consider the converged social engineering attack where an attacker contacts employees by telephone and e-mail to extract different pieces of information about the organization. Then the attacker researches public and private information sources about the organization, and finally attempts to penetrate the organization by entering the facilities, accessing outgoing trash and recycling, or hacking the organization's network. All these activities would be individually designed to gather pieces of information which, on their own, may appear to be isolated or unconnected incidents. However, the shrewd security program with strong security awareness programs and robust technical systems aimed at detecting intrusion attempts will record these potential or real attacks. Individually, however, they only tell part of the story and will only become a strong indicator of an attack when they are combined. If the Chief Information Officer (CIO) hears from the help desk about reports from staff indicating hack attempts, and the Chief Operations Officer (COO) hears about attempted break-ins or dumpster diving, they might not amalgamate this information into a conclusion that a competitor is trying to learn details about the business. Alternatively, if the CSO receives *all* the information, completes an analysis, and presents the aggregate security picture in one presentation to senior management, he or she might deduce the cumulative security risk and be able to take action to counter the attack.

At the beginning of this chapter, I claimed that better-informed senior management can make more prudent decisions. By tracking the positive change in your organization through convergence, you can also support your strategy to converge and give management reassurance throughout the process. As I have indicated a number of times in this book so far, convergence must be slow and measured, and metrics and KPIs can handle most of the measurement. Communicating these measured successes to senior management may need to be ongoing and almost fanatical, especially if there is strong resistance to change.

I have already indicated that by retraining our corporate guard force to conduct desktop IT security policy compliance reviews, in our organization we were able to reduce our IT security policy violations by 54% in three months. Not only did this translate into a significant benefit for the organization, it was real and tangible evidence for senior management that convergence could work and deliver true value. My next message was that, due in part to this increased awareness, the number of stolen laptops was down dramatically over a sustained period. My next convergence message was that by converging the content in security awareness and training material, we have been effectively able to double up on security awareness and security training sessions delivered, because both departments' staff are delivering a common message.

The final step in integrating threat and event report would be to create an algorithm to combine all the threats the organization faces and convert this into a simple communication tool, similar to the Department of Homeland Security's threat color rating system. This would be a quick way to communicate to senior management the current level of risks faced by the organization. In some organizations, you could even make this available at the executive level desktop via a security dashboard whereby the executive could see the relative risk level and investigate the individual threats if necessary. Although this might not be possible in smaller organizations, it could go a long way in communicating that many security threats have already converged and that the organization is faced with their cumulative effects.

# 21

## *Change Management*

Successfully converging security departments is as much about cultural and process change as it is about the collective resources brought to bear for the project. Any astute leader will understand or embrace the concept that you must build the capacity for change in your organization unless the culture is already attuned to ongoing change. Although I understand that these organizations do exist, in my experience they are rare. Understanding the capacity of your organization to change will give you a starting point from which to develop and deliver your new approach. A single leader or a cross-departmental team will need to direct and provide vision to the people affected by the change. It is the dexterous development and communication of a cogent vision that sets the stage for all involved in the change to convergence.

After the corporation-specific vision has been developed, a prudent next step is marshalling the organizational resources and commitment. No project can likely be done without resources, and acquiring resources usually means getting buy-in, building consensus, or spending money. These resources could be IT staff who might need to attend meetings to discuss a potential new security architecture that will affect the network, or company training programs that might have to be altered to incorporate a new, composite security message. A cross-departmental stakeholder group might need to be formed for the development of a new, combined security charter or policy, or an IT planner might need to be consulted for potential impacts to network bandwidth caused by a change from stand-alone analog camera systems to a digital system that will utilize the data network as its transmission medium. All these changes might lead to an intersection with systemic resistance.

It is important to recognize systemic challenges and engage them early on in this process. I chose carefully to say "recognize" rather than "address" the challenges because experience has taught me that not all systemic issues can be resolved. They might be so ingrained in the organizational culture that they cannot be changed. It might then be best to try and work around them or abandon this portion of the conversion in its current form because you can burn up a lot of resources and time trying to beat unresolvable systemic challenges. Systemic challenges can come in many forms, but often appear as structure, policy and process, and HR issues. Structural issues can be a large impediment to converging departments if physical security and IT security reside in different business units that are disinclined to relinquish control of their functions. Senior leaders are often unwilling to surrender control of a department or function within their control because they see this as a loss of a piece of their empire or their span of control. Although you may be able to make a valid argument for the relocation of a function to another business group, this can be a stumbling block for change if the leader will not capitulate.

Systemic challenges that involve policy and process can be significant rivals for change because they often involve the old chestnut "That is the way we have always done it." This adversary of change is a bitter rival because it may involve the editing or revocation of a previous policy or process, which in most organizations is no small matter. For example, if an organization has numerous business units that all have processes and mechanisms to track security incident data, and a new centralized system is proposed, there may be considerable resistance to the dismantling or even sharing of departmental data and systems. Departments can take an almost proprietary view of their internal data.

Another very real systemic challenge to change might come in the form of HR issues such as compensation, pay bands, or union restrictions. I referred earlier in the book to an organization that had combined its physical security control room staff with its IT security monitoring function. They had to retrain employees, change job descriptions, and adjust compensation. Although the retraining and job description changes were reasonably straightforward activities, compensation adjustments involved a significant effort to reclassify certain jobs to a higher pay band in the company pay band structure. Now this was probably no small feat, to say the least, and if it had been an environment with a collective agreement in place it could have taken considerably longer to make the changes, if they could be made at all.

In another organization I know of, the security leadership tried to use incentive programs to motivate security staff from both departments to take training and learn new skills. They offered paid training days, free training, and cross-training opportunities to work on convergence projects. They also offered to send security staff to relevant security conferences where they could be introduced to a broad spectrum of security devices and experiences. The program faltered when the union representing the security workers made claim that the new training and experience would require all the employees in that category to be compensated at a higher level. The sustained operating budget impact of this position by the union was not feasible, so the program ceased. Systemic issues are real, significant, and must be planned for in the process of enabling any change.

At the risk of reiterating too much, I say again that convergence requires slow and measured change. Managing change will require you to measure the progress of convergence and religiously communicate these positive results to all levels of the organization. I cannot overemphasize the need to institutionalize this change by zealous communication of success, extensive management of the details, and meticulous relationship management with the staff and stakeholders involved in the convergence. To summarize, then, this process of change requires one key piece to succeed: A leader!

The strategic leader and change agent will be the one principal figure who drives change, engages and resolves problems, and calms fears related to change. This role requires force of will and personality—someone with the energy and passion to make and defend a powerful rationale for change, the credibility within the organization to marshal the required resources, and the intelligence and wisdom to guide the process through the challenges faced.

The method I have successfully used to build capacity for change is what I call the "top-down and bottom-up" approach. This approach equally distributes the energy and resources dedicated to communicating change and the project successes between the leadership and the staff. The need for change must be supported from above (even driven from the lofty heights of the C-level offices), but the staff of the organization must have input into the tactics used to implement the vision for them to buy into the changes. I am not suggesting that you survey 10,000 staff members, but I do recommend that staff from stakeholder groups be consulted before announcing plans to make significant changes to policy, process, and organizational structure. This is only good management practice, yet it is often forgotten when deadlines become tight or resources become constricted. For sustained change to occur, the average person will usually need to understand why it is important specifically to them.

However, it is said that no one person is an island, so it will be critical to build a quality team of professionals who can work together. With your focus on this, all else will follow in your project. Change management, like security, can also be a weakest-link discipline. It has to be balanced with the right leader, the right plan, and the right team. An imprudent leader will isolate the team and management; an ill-conceived plan will deter the conversion's success; and an uncommitted team or a team with insufficient skills will falter in implementation. Although security metrics will tell most of the stories of your success as you go, the resources must be in place to confront the roadblocks to change.

Although successful and sustained change requires expertise, it also requires unrelenting commitment from all team members. Everyone in the team must be onboard with the new direction and vision, or they will have to be jettisoned from the project. Early on in my project, I was faced with this, and although no one likes forcing involuntary turnover, it might be necessary to overcome the resistance to change. The next chapter will address in more detail the issues and strategies for dealing with resistance to change in convergence projects.

# 22

## Resistance

It may be a universal truth that change can be a little unnerving or even scary at the best of times, and when you try to combine different operating cultures, backgrounds, and technical abilities into a new system, it can lead to a gratuitous insurrection. So first let us examine why changes do not always produce the desired outcomes, and sometimes lead to disaster.

## 1. THE CHANGE IS NOT TIED TO OVERALL STRATEGY

In Chapter 21 I discussed the necessity of having a cogent strategy and vision for your convergence plan. One of the key pieces of this plan's success is that the change must be tied to the overall convergence strategy. If you have made an eloquent case for convergence and have received senior management, staff, and team buy-in, they all must know how the proposed change will aid the convergence plan—how the planned change will move the project ahead. If you are planning to change any job descriptions, pay bands, or reporting structures, it will be crucial to ensure that you thwart the rumor mill and that all affected stakeholders understand the reason for this change. They must see the clear link between this change and the overall strategy—in effect, how this change will enable the overall convergence project and the associated benefits. So although change might occur, if it is not viewed clearly as being linked to the overall project it might not be seen as a stepping stone to a better place. It is critical to eliminate the seeds of doubt at any point in the project which can start passive resistance or anxiety.

## Tips to Overcome

Link change activities directly to the convergence plan and, where possible, link the convergence plan directly to the strategic objectives of the organization. For example, if the new project is focused on converting the analog camera infrastructure to digital and utilizing the data network as the transport method, make sure it is clear to stakeholders that this will cut costs and increase efficiency, and show how this is congruent with the organization's strategic object of cost control and efficiency gains. The overt linkage, even when it might be seemingly obvious, reduces the opportunity for people to make up their own explanations.

## 2.   THE CHANGE PROCESS SUFFERS FROM A LACK OF LEADERSHIP

Although this might seem obvious to all, leadership needs to be sustained throughout the project, but during long-term projects it is not uncommon for leaders, stakeholders, or project sponsors to change. The ability to sustain the conversion plan over the long-term will be directly linked to the rigorous leadership of the project. If strong leadership is not present, the project can falter or lose momentum.

## Tips to Overcome

Bringing team members into a more cohesive organization with one strategic mission and consistent goals will encourage collaboration which, in turn, will help break down some of the walls that can exist between people who previously had prime allegiance to their individual security function. The leader must provide strong direction to new team members but also be compassionate about the fear and concerns felt by the staff. Finally, leaders should always be watching for development opportunities for their team members, to allow for a transition option if the leader leaves the organization.

## 3. INSTITUTIONAL MEMORY IS BLOCKING THE CHANGE

Although your organization might not have tried convergence in the past, the failures of other change projects can affect the resistance to change in your present project. In other words, if an organization has attempted a number of significant change projects and many of them were unsuccessful, this could impact the type and volume of resistance your project encounters. I know of one organization that converged its security groups and then de-converged them because it did not work for them. This will make the next attempt, if ever tried, much more difficult and will require careful planning to achieve success. This institutional memory is buried in the culture of the organization. If you are faced with this, it will be benefit your project if you understand it and have a strategy in your plan to overcome it.

### Tips to Overcome

Overcoming previous organizational problems might be a losing battle, so start by setting realistic goals about convergence. Guide team members in learning to communicate about their shared challenges and help them realize that they share a common language— the language of risk. Keep a keen eye open for cultural issues, such as technobabble, which can drive a wedge between technophiles and the less technically trained.

## 4. INTERNAL POLITICAL REALITIES

Often the internal political realities of the organization do not support (and might even derail) the change process. Maintaining commitment throughout the organizational change and the cyclical shifts in the project funding and priorities can be very challenging for any leader. These realities must be managed (and anticipated, if possible) so that the project is not sidelined or intercepted by these shifting priorities.

## Tips to Overcome

Work with your senior management sponsor to locate any upcoming shifts in political and financial priorities. Communicate all successes rigorously to senior management, but especially where financial or risk reduction benefits are achieved. The more relevant and public your benefits are, the less likely you are to be derailed.

### 5.   PROJECT COMPLEXITY

The age old KISS principle (keep it simple, stupid) has never been more incontrovertible than when applied to change. Trying to attain too much change with extravagant objectives can be deadly to maintaining commitment from team members. Overloading teams with excessive work deliverables and tight deadlines will not improve the opportunity for success. As I have said many times in this book, convergence change needs to be slow and measured. Many organizations have numerous change projects ongoing, including IT, HR, outsourcing, new acquisitions, and a host of other new realities. It is my belief that people have a limit on how much change they can absorb, and prudent leaders will recognize times of intense change across the organization and adapt their strategy accordingly.

## Tips to Overcome

Adaptation takes energy. Other projects or organizational change might be occurring simultaneously but, if you institutionalize it well, set realistic goals, and report success early and consistently, you will lower your risks.

### 6.   FEAR

I believe that one of the most powerful motivators in life is fear, and with any change often comes a certain degree of fear. This can take the form of fear of job loss, fear of having insufficient knowledge for the new environment, and fear of technology, to name just a few.

Although some fear may be irrational, it can lead people to behave in ways unintended by the change.

## Tips to Overcome

You must train, support, and lead your teams. If *you* believe they can complete the tasks, and the tasks are achievable, then you can succeed. You must begin by building a common platform for all to work from. If there are large technical skill gaps among team members, you will need to pair them up on projects where they can learn from each other. You might choose to start with projects where the less technically trained practitioners lead a nontechnical project to invest in their confidence and build trust. To overcome fear, communication will be the key to your success; staff must have a safe environment in which to learn.

## 7.   PERCEPTION

Perception can be reality in the eye of the beholder, and if that beholder is a convergence stakeholder, the perception can make or break the project. If the project is seen as just the latest and greatest fad, a quick fix, or a half-baked approach to business problems, resistance might appear quickly. The risk of having your convergence project seen with a short-term perspective is real and can impact long-term organizational support.

## Tips to Overcome

As stated earlier but cannot be overemphasized, you must clearly communicate your goals, objectives, and strategy to all levels of the organization. Communicate all positive results and do it often. Explain the long-term benefits to the organization and institutionalize them to all stakeholders. Challenge any public statements of resistance with solid success facts and religiously communicate long-term project goals.

## 8.   RIGID CHANGE DESIGN

The environment of business is full of external and internal shifts of opposition. Projects designed with extremely tight time frames or dogmatic implementation schedules risk being in constant conflict. In my experience, projects that are constantly in conflict are some of the first to lose priority support. Be fluid in your scheduling, and you will find the project process far less stressful; there are more important battles to win than the time table.

## Tips to Overcome

Embrace a slow, measured, and steady change schedule. As I stressed earlier, capture wins early from low-hanging fruit projects. With this tactic you can build the capacity to shift projects to take advantage of environmental factors.

## 9.   LACK OF METRICS EXTOLLING RESULTS

Although management will often support a well-written and well-argued strategy, at some point they will likely want to see documented results specifically relevant to their organizational goals. Projects without verifiable metrics run the risk of losing their long-term support or being cast off as making insufficient headway. It is important to solidify progress with regular, documented results to build credibility and validity for continued support.

## Tips to Overcome

Frequently and consistently measure and report to senior management all metrics and key performance indicators that matter to them—cost savings or avoidance, risk reduction, increased compliance levels, reduced cycle time, increased efficiency, and other project benefits. Link project successes to the original convergence plan to validate the original rationale for justifying the project. In researching this book, I spoke with many security professionals from both the physical and IT security fields to discuss what they considered some of the challenges for change when it comes to converging processes, duties, and responsibilities. Here are the most common reasons given by interviewees, in no particular order:

- *Comfort zone.* Interviewees suggested that it is easier for people to stay where they are, that change is challenging, and that there is always an omnipresent fear of failing at something new. Change contests the comfort zone of employees and, although many employees faced with organizational and business changes are interested in learning new skills, a significant percentage of them have been performing essentially the same function for a considerable time. If that comfort zone can be protected and maintained, they can dissuade or even thwart the change by passive and active resistance. A pertinent anecdote about change comes from the story of the Spanish explorer Hernando Cortez. Once he and his crew reached the New World, he had his men burn their ships, thus motivating them to move forward and succeed. Key employees wanting to negatively affect change have been known to be passively resistant by taking blocks of vacation or sick leave, or actively resistant by making unsupportable union challenges, participating in ad hoc debating, or by outright defiance of the new direction. In essence, evolution meets revolution.

- *Slippery slope*. Some responders said that convergence can be seen by staff as the slippery slope to outsourcing. Once jobs have been combined and changed, the next step is to outsource the entire function. Although this fear might not be completely irrational, it is unlikely, in my opinion, to be a convergence strategy adopted in many organizations.
- *Not smart enough*. Deep down in a place where one does not often visit and never speaks about, some practitioners feel insufficiently capable of handling and mastering this new technology. Technology has been an incremental but unrelenting influence on the workplace and many have chosen not to actively engage in the learning process, whereas others have learned only as much as is necessary to perform their jobs. This knowledge gap, although a real problem for many people, is compounded by insufficient training programs for mature working professionals to learn the fundamentals of technology.
- *No perceived need*. Although this was not a common response, more than one person suggested that they did not have to engage in convergence because it was only a fad

and would be gone within months. Given the advance of technology, the integration of security systems, and the continuing pressure to reduce costs, I am confident that convergence is here to stay. We might not call it convergence in a few years, but it will soon be the "new normal."

- *Organizational structure.* One of the most common challenges I heard was the incompatibility of convergence with customary vertical silos and reporting structures. I discussed this concept in Chapter 21 and believe it can be overcome by a dynamic leader armed with a strong business case.
- *Lack of supporting business case materials.* Although only mentioned by one practitioner, I think that in reality this might be one of the most pervasive challenges to convergence. With any new specialization there needs to be academic research, case studies, industry studies, metrics, and other supporting materials to aid practitioners in justifying the adoption of a market-leading position such as convergence. As with all new fields of study, these will come with time and adoption by business.

# 23

# *Lessons Learned About Convergence*

Although the lessons learned, presented in this chapter, are really only my experience and are from essentially one organization, they do represent much of the research I did during the writing of this book. Here are the concrete lessons learned through the initial year of our organization's convergence program.

## PICK THE LOW-HANGING FRUIT

The low-hanging fruit projects are the opportunities to complete natural convergence projects that do not require large capital investment or significant organizational change. They aid the process by building team support and belief in the vision. If any team members have early doubt, they will buy into the program more completely once the team has achieved these initial successes.

## VISION

Make sure that you have at least a working version of the vision for your convergence plan. Even if your initial vision is to only tackle the low-hanging fruit, having a documented and communicated vision that achieves success will add to departmental credibility and build support for future, more enterprise-encompassing projects.

## COMMUNICATION

The successes must be communicated religiously to all levels of the organization. Organizational barriers are broken down by presenting, in concrete terms, evidence that the program can deliver the results as promised—lower overall costs, reduced risk, and increased efficiency, among other benefits.

## CONVERGENCE STRATEGY

It is essential to accept that not every part of every group is best converged, and to concentrate on identifying where the convergence opportunities are authentic and working them into your convergence plan. During the research for this book, I heard from several people that they could not converge a department or a function for some valid reason; however, when asked about other potential convergence activities, ideas quickly emerged. To reduce frustration and wasted resources, accept that there may be some functions that just cannot be converged initially or ever. Keep your focus on the projects that will work, and take as much convergence as will work for your organization.

## EAT YOUR YOUNG EARLY, WHEN THEY ARE JUICY AND TENDER

Systemic or organizational issues are likely to arise in any convergence or change project. It is important to address these system issues early because they can have significant impacts on your chances of sustained success. Project sponsorship, senior management support, known or suspected resistance points, budget issues, policy and process roadblocks, or general structural or silo design conflicts must be engaged early on. If these issues are engaged or addressed early, you will have the time and ability to react or make changes to your overall plan. If you anticipate resistance from a union or a functional department, it might be best to pull back from convergence-related projects and concentrate on other projects while you determine a resolution to these roadblocks. No matter what, you will not regret engaging systemic problems early, as long as you continue to produce results and you communicate those results.

## CREATIVITY IS CRUCIAL

Although the cliché that every organization is different might have some truth, most organizations have factors that are unique to them, including competitive position, profitability, compliance issues, business cycle position, favorable management, and external threat environment. It is those factors that allow for the creative analysis and design. Although many of the opportunities I have discussed in this book are potential opportunities for every organization, there are undoubtedly many other potential convergence projects out there, across the variety of corporations and government units. They are not discovered by one all-knowing, all-seeing leader locked in a room with this book. Such opportunities will emerge when an enthusiastic team is brought together, sharing enterprise security risk issues and looking for ways to attain the benefits from combined risk mitigation tactics.

## EDUCATION AND TRAINING

Because convergence is a foray into new territory for many practitioners, and involves security professionals learning new skills and understanding different threats, it is critical that education and training play a role in developing a convergence program. Although asking for creativity is a reasonable request, it is also pragmatic to equip team members with new knowledge through education, training, and, most significantly, cross-training. Some of the most significant results our projects achieved occurred when people stepped out of their comfort zone while applying their knowledge to the problems of other security groups or functions.

## CHANGE MANAGEMENT

Change management is absolutely crucial for cross-departmental projects. The issues discussed in Chapter 21, such as culture, process, and marshaling resources, were battlefield-tested during our project and by others included in my research. These issues represent opportunities which, once engaged, will help reduce conflict and optimize project success.

## EMOTIONAL SUSTAINMENT

As mentioned in an earlier chapter, a leader and his or her force of will can move a project forward. The leader needs to design and deploy a pragmatic vision, religiously communicate to all levels of the organization, engage and overcome resistance, develop a professional team, and execute the plan. During this process there can be many factors that challenge the success of this plan and sustainment of the results; it is the motivating and driven leadership of the CSO or project leader that will maintain consistency of commitment within the project team members.

## JETTISON THE DEADWOOD

If you have determined that convergence is the future for your organization, having fully qualified, motivated, and supportive team members who support your vision is crucial to your success. As a leader faced with a team member who is either opposed to or too rigid in their attitude toward the new security vision, you might need to "jettison the deadwood" and find a dedicated replacement. Although it is neither pleasant nor desirable, it will indicate to the other team members your unwavering commitment and illustrate your resolve to complete the new vision. Convergence is a strategic activity; it entails evolving your organization's security program to the next level of integration.

# *Wrapping it All Up*

# 24

# *The Case for Security and Convergence*

Much of the challenge in making a business case for any security issue is how the function of security is positioned in the organization. For countless years, security professionals on both sides of the aisle have relied on or reverted to the age-old chestnut "The sky will fall if you don't do this," or the FUD factor. This fear we instill in our senior leaders might get us the funding we seek in the short term, but it does very little to develop that professional C-suite relationship with our management team. In fact, I would argue that you can only go to the well so many times without an incident occurring before management will begin to disbelieve the risk as being legitimate or as acute as was presented in the case.

The real problem here is that the risk might be very real the next time, but "The boy has cried 'wolf' too many times, so the villagers just don't come." I have been just as guilty of this as the next security manager, and sometimes this reaction is appropriate. However, it often leads to senior management viewing security strictly as a tactical function—not capable of strategic leadership—

and they will henceforth only fund initiatives that represent large potential losses or significant compliance breaches. This is the main problem with persuasion arguments based only on risk: There is no way to accurately predict when the serious incident might occur.

Security managers who are trying to deal with executives who have an "It won't happen to us" mentality are probably plagued with an inability to sell the FUD approach. In the wake of September 11th, many would claim that this FUD approach represents a valid argument. But even now in parts of the United States, Canada, and even other countries that have less appeal as a terrorist target, security's internal corporate profile is returning to its pre-9/11 state as the economy and business drivers once again begin to take center stage in business decision-making.

The way in which security managers and leaders justify their budgets and get support for strategies such as convergence in the future can be greatly enhanced by understanding how company executives evaluate the entire organization. Further, by learning to speak the language of business, security professionals can clearly enunciate—in business terms—the value the security function truly brings to the organization.

For many years security departments have pondered how to best defend their value to the organization, and often have struggled to simply preserve their resources. We know that in high-security environments where security is seen as a mission-critical component to an operation (for example, NASA[‡]), security budget challenges might be less vigorous than at the local office tower where security plays an integral but arguably less conspicuous role. The same is true in IT security. When protecting government information or trade secrets, the security mandate might be clear, but protecting customers' personal information in a database might get attention. In this environment, the security manager might struggle to identify and encapsulate all the value his or her department affords the organization.

This may be because the business terms of reference are not absolutely familiar to the security manager. Many times, the measurements used to evaluate the security function are incident-related versus business-related. Often, what is subjectively measured is

---

[‡]The author has no actual knowledge of the security budget challenges at NASA. This is offered as a example and is based on speculation and opinion.

whether incidents have or have not occurred. Often, the absence of incidents engenders a feeling that either security must be doing its job or that nothing ever really happens. The well-documented problem with this view is that business executives are disinclined to increase funding to "nothing." Further, awareness of the security department's value can sometimes be subdued because of its own nature. The security function utilizes tools such as access control, need-to-know basis, least privileges, and other information- and knowledge-controlling tactics. By their very nature, they control what information is widely understood across the organization. This is a key restrictor of communicating security's internal value.

One useful technique is to embrace an integrated and immutable approach to enunciating the total value provided by the enterprise security departments to the organization, *delivered in business terms*. To do this, let us look at the strategic management concept of the organization's value chain.

According to Michael E. Porter, "The primary analytical tool of strategic cost analysis is a value chain identifying the separate activities, functions and business processes that are performed in designing, producing, marketing, delivering, and supporting a product or service."[1] The value chain diagram in Figure 24-1 represents the typical primary and secondary activities of businesses. This particular example is focused more on a product-based environment but the process is the same for service environments.

This chain represents the individual activities undertaken by an organization that together create a product for or service to the

**Figure 24-1**    Security value chain.

customer. The value chain diagram includes a profit component and might not always be part of the discussion, such as when evaluating a nonprofit or not-for-profit organization.

The desegregation of the company's value-creating functions allows for a clear view of the firm's cost structure, and is thus an indispensable management tool. It also provides the security manager an opportunity to clearly articulate the significance of the security department's contribution throughout the organization. This is especially helpful in larger firms where the security function may be business unit-independent or geographically dispersed.

Hence, the task at hand is to reevaluate the way the security function is presented internally to:

- Aid in creating awareness of the value and services security provides,
- Communicate the value created and services performed in each value chain component,
- Identify the critical business-enabling functions that are actually performed by security to the benefit of the organization, and
- Ensure that management understands this value created by security.

Let us therefore look at each component of the value chain. We will examine:

- The typical activities performed in each link of the value chain,
- How the security function enables the business, and
- What the result is for the business.

The following section on the value chain identifies some of the potential value-creating activities in a generic operation. It is not meant to be an exhaustive list by any means, but it illustrates a few of the value-creating functions security often performs.

## Unbundling the Security Function

***Primary Activities***[2]    Purchased supplies and inbound logistics.

**Activities Performed**   Activities, costs, and assets associated with purchasing raw materials, components, and organizational supplies; consumer goods, receiving, warehousing, distributing, and inventory management.

**How Does the Security Function Enable Business?**   Ensuring consistent and secure access to the premises by vendors, suppliers, and trucking and delivery firms is a major supply chain priority. Key processes where security enables these activities, such as CCTV and access control systems, need to be highlighted. The secure working environment where raw materials and finished products are delivered and moved through the enterprise is enabled by security. Automated security control equipment tracks packages through the system and reduces the opportunities for shrinkage; physical protection of warehouse space reduces the chances of theft. Increased reliability of inventory reduces overhead costs due to shrinkage, increases inventory turn speed, and increases the likelihood that customers will receive the products or services they expect on time, every time.

**Result**   Positive impact on the bottom line; efficient and profitable business is enabled by the security function.

## Operations

**Activities Performed**   Activities, costs, and assets associated with converting inputs into final product or services: production assembly, packaging, equipment maintenance, facilities, quality assurance, and environmental protection.

**How Does the Security Function Enable Business?**   Operations require a smooth transition of products or services through the company while moving throughout the production and/or development environments. Secure environments ensure that inputs are available as needed to complete operations. Finished products can then be completed on time and deliveries to customers can be conveyed as promised. Reputation is enhanced by the increased reliability of being able to deliver quality products and services continuously. IT security ensures that the network is protected and free from malicious software that could cause downtime in production systems.

Security enhances a safe workplace where employees feel protected from harm or workplace violence, free from preventable physical hazards, and equipped with useful, appropriate, and reliable emergency response equipment and plans, and promotes a productive and satisfactory work environment.

**Result**    Positive impact on the bottom line; efficient, reliable and profitable operations are enabled by the security function.

## Distribution and Outbound Logistics

**Activities Performed**    Activities, costs, and assets associated with physical distribution of products or services to buyers (finished goods warehousing, order processing, picking, packing, shipping, delivery vehicle operations, and establishing and maintaining a dealer/distributor network).

### How Does the Security Function Enable Business?    Similar to purchased supplies and inbound logistics, a secure and controlled environment promotes a viable business atmosphere and optimizes the profit potential. A secure environment reduces shrinkage and involuntary losses, which adds value directly to the bottom line.

Many organizations set standards for employee conduct through detailed organizational policy. The rights and responsibilities of employees and security departments are articulated in corporate security policy and procedures. A detailed and thorough security policy is a statement of intent and guidance by senior management to the organization as a whole regarding the commitment, ownership, responsibilities, processes, and other themes applicable to security. It promotes consistency and understanding across the organization and sets boundaries for employee behavior. This provides for a dependable, repeatable, and verifiable workplace environment that encourages efficiency and effectiveness. IT security enables proficient and network infrastructure to electronically communicate with and share data with distributors, vendors, and third parties. Transactions with financial institutions are completed in a safe and confidential manner.

The investigation functions aid in tracking and retrieving misplaced, misappropriated, and converted company resources. This function obtains key evidence to be used in identifying dishonest persons in the organization so that lost or converted resources can be retrieved and potential future losses can be prevented.

**Result**   Positive impact on the bottom line; efficient, reliable, and profitable operations are enabled by the security function. Costs are reduced and future risks are managed.

## Sales and Marketing

**Activities Performed**   Activities, costs, and assets associated with sales force efforts, advertising and promotion, market research and planning, and dealer/distribution support.

**How Does the Security Function Enable Business?**   The sales and marketing functions of a business deal with the development, management, and dissemination of information, much of it proprietary, sensitive, and of strategic competitive advantage to the firm. Security policy protects information through asset classification and control. Security mechanisms designed to protect sensitive or confidential company information are engaged and risk assessments assist in allocating security mechanisms to address potential threat events, such as intelligence gathering, espionage, or even inadvertent disclosure by an employee.

Protection of intellectual property is maintained through physical and IT security controls put in place in response to threat and risk assessment, and actual security incidents. Marketing data such as customer and sales numbers are protected in physically controlled IT hardware and locked filing cabinets.

**Result**   Positive impact on the bottom line; information is protected and potential competitive advantage is maintained. Profit potential is enhanced by the security function.

## Customer Service

**Activities Performed**   Activities, costs, and assets associated with providing assistance to buyers such as installation, spare parts delivery, maintenance and repair, technical assistance, buyer inquiries, and complaints.

***How Does the Security Function Enable Business?*** The ability to provide service operations flows from having a reliable environment in which to work. The security function avails ready access to replacement parts (which are actually there, not removed or stolen) and ready access to service vehicles (which have been protected and not vandalized). Often security deals with customer inquiries or complaints after hours, either on the phone or in person. The impressions formed in these interactions are often integral to the way a customer views the business.

***Result*** Positive impact on the bottom line; efficient, reliable, and profitable operations are enabled by the security function. Positive impact on customer relations.

## Support Activities: Research, Technology, and Systems Development

***Activities Performed*** Activities, costs, and assets associated with product research and development (R&D), process systems, computer-aided design (CAD) and engineering, and computer support systems.

***How Does the Security Function Enable Business?*** Physical, logical, and technological controls of R&D and technology assets protect secret or proprietary information. Often, this proprietary information is the sole source of competitive advantage for a firm, and its loss would be catastrophic for the organization. Protection of R&D environments increases the ability to maintain secrecy of new company assets and potential future strategic competitive advantage.

Security provides a safe, reliable, and verifiable environment. Audit trails and access control technology allow for ability to ensure authorization and authentication activities.

***Result*** Positive impact on the bottom line; information is protected and potential competitive advantage is maintained. Profit potential is enhanced by the security function.

## Human Resource Management

***Activities Performed*** Activities, costs, and assets associated with recruitment, hiring, training, development, and compensation of all types of personnel; labor relation activities; and development of knowledge base, skills, and core competencies.

***How Does the Security Function Enable Business?*** Probably one of the more dynamic security interactions is related to people. Security activities start at the initial introduction of new personnel into the organization. New employees are institutionalized into the firm via their entry activities, which include new employee security orientation. New employees receive security policy information, procedures, and standards to which they must comply. A clear and cogent understanding is established from Day One, which creates recognition in the employee's mind that the company takes security seriously. This can increase employee confidence in the company and the security controls that are in place to deter misbehavior. With increasing difficulties in attracting and retaining quality employees and the increasing costs of voluntary turnover, ensuring that employees feel safe in the workplace is essential.

Security training and security awareness programs aid employees in detecting potential loss events, which can then be addressed with efficiency and confidence. Further, such programs remind employees to protect company property and information from potential loss or disclosure.

Employee screening and background checks performed by security departments can identify suspect histories in potential applicants, thereby eliminating a potential problem employee before he or she is hired. This can reduce costs and potential losses in many follow-on issues or loss events.

Labor unrest and strike actions are observed for and protected against by security departments. Employee action is monitored and recorded for the protection of employees, management, and company assets.

Security and special investigation unit departments handle investigations and internal theft complaints. Management might not have the skills or experience for conducting such investigations, performing interviews, and ensuring custody of evidence used in terminations and criminal prosecutions. Security is often successful in recovering lost assets.

Employee terminations are carried out with the support of security. Security departments profile high-risk former employees and police departments are contacted where physical risk or harm might occur from a volatile employee termination. Very often, security departments will undertake the retrieval of company property from former employees or assist in company property being retrieved from the former employee before they leave the premises.

**Result**    Positive impact on the bottom line; increased security awareness, potential losses reduced or prevented, and recoveries made. More confident staff reduces turnover costs and improves the view of the company as an employer of choice.

## General Administration

**Activities Performed**    Activities, costs, and assets relating to general management, accounting, finance, legal and regulatory affairs, safety and security, management information systems (MIS), strategic alliances and strategic partner collaboration, and other overhead functions.

**How Does the Security Function Enable Business?**    In the organizational structure, security is often relegated to general administration. Many important functions are performed here that can be expanded upon. Risk management in general is a management function, but often has significant input from security departments. Completing risk assessments comes with a clear understanding of the environmental risks present. Often security is the best-equipped department to provide such information or is most closely in touch with it. Risk management decisions pertaining to business investments in foreign nations are often supported by country risk assessments from security. Background checks of potential acquisition targets and or collaborative partners with whom proprietary technology or processes may be shared can identify potential competitive issues or dubious backgrounds.

Executive protection details ensure the safety of key officers, employees, and executives. The loss of these personnel could have a significant impact on the organization; the presence of these personnel creates a stable and reliable work environment for all. The loss of specific expertise in a technical discipline, say through the kidnapping of a scientist or researcher, could introduce all kinds of financial, personal, competitive, and organizational trouble to the workplace.

Internal audit processes assist in the uncovering of misappropriated funds or, alternatively, increase the level of assurance in the company financial systems. Internal forensic investigations help determine which assets have been utilized and for what purposes. In the case of assets being used for inappropriate or nefarious purposes, custody of evidence can be maintained for legal and civil proceedings.

**Result**    Positive impact on the bottom line; increased level of corporate assurance; protection of key employees and officers.

## EXPECTED IMPACT OF THIS APPROACH

By adopting the value chain approach to evaluating and communicating security contributions to an organization, security managers can direct numerous new learning and communication opportunities. First, security managers can facilitate a greater understanding by senior management of how security actually enables business at each step in the business process. Next, security managers can increase senior management's understanding of what security does and why this is important in making decisions on future budget and resource allocations. This creates an opportunity for free-flowing dialogue on important issues that can often be sensitive or of grave concern to the organization. If we learned anything from September 11th, it is that security needs to be an important and necessary, integrated component of all organizations. The question that remains is: How do security managers ensure that the awareness of security criticality keeps moving forward? The answer might indeed be to use an organization-specific value chain to demonstrate how security enables the business.

## Transforming Perception of the Organizational Security Role

Often, security is seen as just another department in the overall organization. A key challenge for security managers—and what the value chain seeks to do—is change the perception of department heads and employees to one where security interacts and enables all units of the organization.

Figure 24-2 represents the visual shift in perception from a mindset that sees security as a homogeneous business unit that is a cost center for the organization, to a centric business-enabling function that aids in revenue creation and loss reduction across the enterprise.

## Profit Margin

It can be said that all functions within an organization contribute to the overall profit of the business in some way. Here, we have seen how security can contribute to the overall profit margin of an organization by enabling productivity, effectiveness, and efficiency, reducing organizational losses, and managing the long-term risk of the enterprise. Whether it is facilitating material and personnel organizational efforts, aiding in the maintenance and management

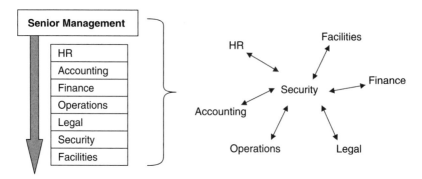

**Figure 24-2** Transformation of perception.

of organizational resources, or protecting the physical and information resources of the business, security has a role to play in each area as a contributor to enterprise profitability.

The value actually created in this approach is that security and business managers can finally begin to speak a common language. Security managers from around the world have struggled to encapsulate the value they create for an organization, and then accurately and efficiently convey that value to senior management in such a way that it is received and understood with its appropriate magnitude. At a time when the security function is at its most elevated importance to many organizations in years, this approach allows security managers to bridge the business language communication gap to senior management and to fully communicate their department's paramount organizational importance.

Although return on investment (ROI) may be a commonly debated measure for determining the worthiness of a project in private-sector organizations, I caution the reader that it may not always be the best measurement for convergence projects. There might be ROI in numerous technology projects or in any projects that reduce overall headcount in the organization, but linking security project goals and success to enablement of the business goals and infrastructure should resonate well with business professionals.

Making a case for convergence might be possible using the FUD factor, but you will probably not be able to sustain serious structural reorganization and technological change this way. Selling security today requires that security professionals clearly communicate the value of security in terms of the business functions that create and sustain revenue or enhance business worth. The process of linking the types of benefits identified in this book to your organization's security value chain, and clearly enunciating how convergence will further optimize the enterprise security endeavor of your organization, is a robust business strategy and is likely to be received as such.

## REFERENCES

1.   Thompson, A. A., Strickland, A. J., editors. (2001). *Strategic Management, Concepts and Cases,* 12th ed. New York: McGraw-Hill.
2.   Porter, M. E. (1985). Concepts of the value chain. *Competitive Advantage.* New York: The Free Press; pp. 37–43.

# 25

## *A Model for Moving Forward*

There are probably many models you could utilize to move ahead with a convergence vision. You could select the creeping incrementalism approach discussed in this book, which optimizes benefits and change management with organizational culture. You could choose to adopt an opportunistic approach that focuses on enhancing training and building infrastructure, and then engage convergence projects only when the timing was right. There certainly is an argument for adopting the Big Bang approach and moving to convergence in one concentrated effort, although I do not recommend it without having an experienced convergence professional on your team, as discussed in Chapter 19.

The City of Vancouver approached the convergence of IT and physical security in the manner primarily described in this book, and that paid many dividends for the security program and the organization. You could argue that the leadership, resources, and timing were sufficiently harmonious because of the lead-up to the 2010 Winter Olympics, and that this presented a unique situation.

But, in fact, this was not the case; it was more about having a professional with the right skills, in an organization that has a management team willing to show leadership on a strategic issue and sufficient dedicated resources to achieve the transition.

The ability of security groups to fully leverage existing technology infrastructure for organizational benefits and cost savings will be a key, defining factor in an organization's strategic orientation in the coming years. The initial integration points for security convergence exist at the strategic, tactical, policy, and operational levels.

At the strategic level, focus is on integrated security strategy development and cost saving opportunities. This can come in the form of one enterprise security strategy that provides leadership for enterprise issues. An example of this is reducing duplication in identity management systems by integrating both into one system, similar to the process being done at Boeing and other large organizations grappling with the requirements of Homeland Security Presidential Directive 12. Other strategic issues include budget harmonization and capital rationing.

At the tactical level, opportunities exist in merging risk assessment and investigation methodologies as well as in developing specialty-integrated training programs for more effective staff performance. In the City of Vancouver, the investigations and risk assessment methodologies are integrated to ensure that these activities take advantage of all available skill sets and knowledge bases to reduce duplication and cycle time in completing the activities. Further, costs are reduced by only completing one threat and risk assessment for a facility, instead of one physical and one IT.

At the policy level, you can minimize policy duplication by integrating similar physical and IT security policy subjects into a single policy development. If you are developing a corporate standard on access control, consider all forms of access to the organization, both IT and physical, and then develop a policy that addresses the protection of and access to all corporate assets. The policy cycle time savings could be as high as 50%, and this will significantly reduce the time in which stakeholders have to be engaged for comment and review.

Finally, at the operational level you can integrate security functions for organizational benefits such as utilizing physical security staff to aid in IT security policy compliance reviews. Security personnel who are patrolling facilities can be retrained to look for IT security risks at desktop locations and risky conditions such as rogue wireless access points.

To engage security convergence principles in a meaningful way, one must divorce oneself from the concept of discrete security factions, and begin to allocate integrated resources to mitigate organizational risk. The overall goal of all security and risk departments is, in the end, appropriate risk mitigation and the protection of the organization's people, information, and property while minimizing the costs of those protections and enabling efficient business delivery for the organization.

Remember to develop a comprehensive security vision and work the plan, subject to the changing external and internal conditions that confront you. When internal political realities shift, be prepared to move with those realities and adjust your plan. While accepting that some parts of the security function may not be best operated in a converged function, manage the message through the process of change and focus on the convergence activities that do produce benefit.

Finally, do not eviscerate what works because of challenges in what does not. Bring the working components together and locate the pieces that deliver value, and support those processes.

## CHECKLIST FOR SECURITY CONVERGENCE

- Get an executive-level sponsor.
- Develop a solid change management plan.
- Lay out the new vision for the team.
- Benchmark wherever you can.
- Be prepared for change management issues and proactively address them.
- Get budget support as early as possible.
- Drive metrics up through the organization early.
- Work the plan; be emotionally supportive and fearless.
- Get senior management buy-in early.
- Conduct a strategic review and inventory of assets.
- Develop business cases.
- Enhance, build, hire, and change people skill sets.

## OTHER REMINDERS

- Build your strategy and integration plan focused on the benefits!
- Engage the common language of risk between groups.
- Implement what you can as soon as possible—pick the strategic, tactical, and operational low-hanging fruit.
- Continue to leverage people, process, and technology for additional success.
- Remember to be creative.

# Index